"Learn from yesterday,
live for today,
hope for tomorrow.
The important thing is to
never stop questioning."

HAPP*ier* HOUR
with
EINSTEIN

Another Round!

ANDRICK
GROUP™

Thinking about Thinking | Learning about Learning

reLEARN:
A Smarter Way to Work®

Copyright © 2018 by Melissa Hughes, Ph.D.

Special gratitude to editors Susan Rooks and Alice Austin and graphic designer, Bradley Keppler.

ISBN: 978-0-692-19025-8

CONTENTS

Introduction

Genius: The word is derived from the Latin verb *gignere* which means 'to generate or bring forth.' The concept of genius originated in ancient Rome. The Romans believed that every male was born with a "genius" and every female was born with a "juno," a "tuletary or moral spirit" assigned to protect them from birth to death. Because each person was born with a divine protector, one's special talents or abilities were ascribed to the genius. Over time, the construct of guiding spirits responsible for intellect evolved to more rational and scientific explanations of mental ability.

Intelligence has long been considered the essence of genius. For centuries, we've grappled with the meaning of intelligence and the best way to measure it. Ancient philosophers questioned the origin and nature of intelligence. Hippocrates believed the brain was the "primary seat of sense and spirit." Aristotle believed that the heart was the most important human organ and the home of intelligence, motion, and sensation. Francis Galton believed that intelligence was genetic, and he dedicated considerable time and energy trying to measure it scientifically.

It wasn't until 1916 when a Stanford psychologist named Lewis Terman introduced the "intelligence quotient" or the IQ test named the *Stanford Revision of the Binet-Simon Scale*. Terman believed that intelligence was genetic and the strongest predictor of success. Unlike Binet and Simon who originally developed the test to identify and provide educational services for struggling students, Terman proposed that his revised test be used to classify children based solely on intelligence to determine an appropriate education and career track. In his opinion, before a child finished primary school, the IQ test would indicate whether the student had the intellect of a doctor or a ditch digger.

In 1921, Terman initiated the *Genetic Studies of Genius*, a longitudinal study that would track children with extremely high IQ through adulthood. Terman administered the test to more than 1,500 students and identified those who had scored in the genius or near genius range. The researchers followed the "Termites," throughout their lives, analyzing educational, professional, and personal achievements. The goal was to determine if IQ would identify the next Albert Einstein, Charles Darwin, or Marie Curie.

Not surprisingly, most of the participants completed college and became highly successful professionals in a wide range of fields such as law, medicine, engineering, physics, literature, and music. But, one of the most significant findings of Terman's research was that intelligence did not guarantee success. A number of the students struggled professionally and personally. Some flunked out of college and/or failed to maintain employment. Others battled addictions to drugs or alcohol. Perhaps the most unexpected discovery was that intelligence does not always predict success. Two students eliminated from the study because they did not score high enough on the IQ test illuminated this finding. Both Luis Alvarez and William Shockley who were not identified as geniuses on the IQ test went on to college, earned doctorate degrees, became physicists and each won a Nobel Prize. Not one of the "Termites" accomplished that recognition.

Ironically, at about the same time that Terman embarked on his study, Dr. Albert Einstein was redefining the word *genius*. Einstein published a little paper about general relativity with his theory of gravitation in 1916, the same year Terman introduced his IQ test. In 1917, Einstein applied the general theory of relativity to model the structure of the universe. In 1921, the same year Terman selected his "Termites" to prove intelligence was an inherited trait, Einstein was awarded the Nobel Prize for Physics for "his services to Theoretical

Physics, and especially for his discovery of the law of the photoelectric effect."

It seems logical, then, that the journey to understand better both brain function and intellectual capacity begins with him. As a child, Albert was remarkably quiet and struggled with language so much that his family feared he would never speak. His primary school teachers described him as lazy, sloppy and even "mentally retarded." He certainly wouldn't have qualified for Terman's genius study, and many questioned whether he'd live a normal life.

How could this child's brain develop into one that would grapple with theoretical problems, unravel cosmic mysteries and discover science that would literally change the world? Thanks to the pathologist who secretly smuggled his brain from the autopsy room, scientists have been exploring that question since 1955.

What would unfold as a bizarre journey for Einstein's brain began with severe chest pains on April 17, 1955. He was admitted to Princeton Hospital and died the next day of an aortic aneurysm. His last will and testament unequivocally instructed his body to be cremated, with the ashes scattered secretly, but an autopsy would be conducted.

Dr. Thomas Harvey was not scheduled to perform the autopsy and prepare the body for cremation. He was the "on-call" pathologist that night as a last-minute replacement. The young Dr. Harvey found himself alone in the morgue looking down at one of the most amazing scientists in history. At that moment, he decided that the world could not and would not be finished learning from the genius.

Dr. Harvey left the hospital that day carrying a duffle bag that contained Einstein's brain as well as his eyeballs which he later gave to Henry Abrams, Einstein's ophthalmologist. Abrams ultimately placed them in a safety deposit box in New York City where they remain to this day. Princeton Hospital urged Harvey to turn over the brain, but he refused. A few months later, he was fired. We can debate all day long about whether Harvey was a hero, opportunist, or criminal, but eventually the Einstein family granted permission to study this amazing brain. In the name of science, Albert's wild ride began.

Harvey was not a brain specialist, and at some point, he realized that he didn't have the skills or the expertise to conduct the study. Harvey sliced Einstein's brain into 240 pieces. He sent small slivers to a handful of the best and brightest neuroscientists around the world and waited for them to report back with their findings. Meanwhile, he guarded the remainder of Einstein's brain as the most significant treasure of the 20th century. As he waited for these hand-picked scientists to unlock the secrets of this great mind, Harvey was both secretive and protective of what would be, according to him, a contribution to science on par with contributions of Einstein himself.

For the next 20 years, little was heard about either the brain or the research. In 1978, 27-year old journalist, Steven Levy, would put both back in the headlines. As it turns out, Levy's editor was fascinated with Einstein and tasked the young reporter with finding out what happened to his brain. Levy's old-school investigative reporting started with a call to 411 which ultimately led him to a Dr. Thomas S. Harvey located in Wichita, Kansas. Levy simply called him up, and the two agreed to meet on a Saturday afternoon in Harvey's little office. Reluctantly, Harvey began to share his story. Then, perhaps overtaken by pride, he revealed that the brain was right there in that tiny office! Behind a Styrofoam beer cooler, inside an old Costa Cider box, and buried under crumpled newspapers was a mason jar that contained gray, spongy chunks of human tissue. Harvey confirmed the contents of the jar were the remains of Einstein's cerebellum, cerebral cortex, and aortic vessels.

After Levy's article was printed later that summer, Harvey's quiet life would be interrupted by a flock of reporters who camped out on his lawn and scientists who wanted in on the research. He became the coach with the first-round draft pick for the international neuroscience dream team as he determined who would play on "Team Einstein."

Dr. Marian Diamond was one of his top draft picks. Harvey cleaned out an empty Kraft Miracle Whip jar and sent four small pieces to the Berkeley neuroscientist by U.S.P.S. By 1984, Dr. Diamond was ready to announce her important discovery to the world. Dr. Einstein had more glial cells than the average brain, especially in the association cortex, that part of the brain responsible for complex thinking and imagination. For a long time, neuroscientists thought that the glial cells were just the brain's maintenance and housekeeping staff, delivering nutrients, repairing neurons, and clearing out all of the dead cells on their way out.

Additional research, however, established that while the neurons get all of the attention for brain activity, glial cells are actually responsible for synapse function. Those tiny gaps between neurons use synapses to communicate and process information. We can thank our glial cells for the information highway system that moves data faster than a Formula I race car.

Now it was all beginning to make sense. Einstein had more glial cells which made his neurons function and communicate better. Obviously, this was big news! Diamond's work gained much attention in the science community. Some celebrated the discovery while others poked holes in it. Despite all the controversy, Diamond's groundbreaking discovery was scrutinized and exposed as critically flawed with selection bias.

Over the next few decades, a select number of respected scientists would have the opportunity to look at Dr. Einstein's brain. We'd learn that his frontal cortex was thinner than average but more neuron-dense. We also learned that Einstein had an extra ridge on his mid-frontal lobe, the part used for complex planning and working memory.

In 1999, Canadian neuroscientist Sandra Witelson published a paper entitled *The Exceptional Brain of Albert Einstein.* In it, Witelson claimed that while Einstein had more glial cells and neurons, the real difference was in the fissure patterns. Albert didn't have much of a lateral fissure. Also called the *Sylvian fissure*, this major furrow separates the parietal lobe and the frontal lobe. Since the parietal lobe handles mathematical ability, spatial reasoning, and three-dimensional visualization while the frontal lobe is responsible for executive functioning, this discovery seemed pretty significant for the guy who envisioned a ride through space on a beam of light and translated it into the theory of relativity.

After safeguarding the brain for over 40 years, Harvey returned to Princeton; however, his odd obsession with Einstein was not over. The 84-year old Harvey and a freelance writer named Michael Paterniti set out on a cross-country road trip to meet Al's granddaughter, Evelyn Einstein. Like some weird spinoff of *Weekend at Bernie's*, Albert's brain sloshed around in a Tupperware container stowed in the trunk of their rented Buick Skylark as they traveled from New Jersey to California. Paterniti chronicles the bizarre excursion in his book, *Driving Mr. Albert: A Trip Across America with Einstein's Brain*. Evelyn didn't want the brain, so the men popped it back in the trunk and returned to Princeton where they would part ways. A year later, fueled by a sense of either guilt or responsibility, Harvey quietly returned Albert's brain to Princeton.

Fast forward to 2013 when team of scientists led by Weiwei Men at East China Normal University's Department of Physics discovered that beyond an abundance of glial cells and a neuron-dense frontal cortex, Dr. Al had a freakishly large corpus callosum. This biggest nerve fiber bundle in the brain connecting the two hemispheres was thicker and larger than normal. An undersized lateral fissure combined with an oversized corpus callosum meant that Einstein's brain was more well-connected than most. He was able to integrate his analytical and methodical left brain with his imaginative and artistic right brain. He was able to imagine what it would be like to accelerate through space on a beam of light where time would slow down, mass would increase, and length would contract. Some scientists believe that this hyper-connected brilliance precipitated the 1905 Annus Mirabilis, the miracle year when he produced four papers that would change everything.

Terman's theory, that intelligence is inherited and the most significant predictor of success, was once widely accepted. Scientists believed that we were born with a certain capacity to learn and that we did the best we could with what we had. Now, we know differently. Since the 1990's, also known as "the Decade of the Brain," we've discovered that we can actually increase our capacity for learning, problem solving, creativity, success, and happiness.

Technological advances and a wealth of research have enabled us to peek inside the brain and see what factors enhance and impede neural growth, connectivity, mental acuity and decline. We all have the same pieces and parts between our ears. Understanding what maximizes cognitive function and what short circuits reasoning, decision making, and rational thought may be what separates the best of us from the rest of us.

Having spent many years teaching students from elementary school to the university level, my professional growth was guided by the premise that

I couldn't master my craft of teaching unless I had a solid understanding of how the human brain learns. Throughout my studies, I filled my cognitive backpack with instructional methods and educational theories that qualified me to teach children what they needed to know to be labeled "proficient" and move on to the next grade.

Unfortunately, none of those courses included how cortisol actually impedes the brain's ability to function properly or how laughter releases dopamine and an array of endorphins that enhance cognition. Such information would have been extremely valuable to have as someone tasked with equipping children with the tools needed for lifelong learning. I always found it curious that in all those years of preparation, no one ever taught me how the brain works, how we actually learn, as well as those factors which impact our capacity for intelligence, problem-solving and creativity.

Since those early days in the classroom, my journey has been guided by the desire to discover more about how the brain works and how to make it work better. This book is a collection of neuroscientific discoveries that explain how that three-pound wrinkly mass between our ears manages our experiences, knowledge, emotions, decisions, achievements, and failures which shape the mental models we create for ourselves and the world around us.

Why do we make irrational decisions or jump to illogical conclusions?
Why do some people avoid challenges while others embrace them?
Why does rejection hurt so much?
Why does laughter feel so good?
How does failure make us smarter?
Why are optimists more successful than pessimists?
Why do we make irrational decisions when we're tired?

Armed with advanced technology, scientists have discovered the answers to these questions and additional explanations about how we learn and think. As we continue to explore the mysteries of the human brain, the very nature of science pushes us to replicate, scrutinize, discover flaws, and test new theories. Undoubtedly, some studies presented here may be challenged with critical examination, additional research, and opposing arguments. The intention is not to substantiate or discredit any particular study, nor is it an exhaustive look at the body of research. This book won't prepare you for a degree in neuroscience, and the content and style are not designed to be that of a scientific paper or medical symposium. Think of it more as happy hour with Einstein and a few other brainiacs sitting around the bar learning about learning and thinking about thinking.

Cheers!

Section I

Learning about Learning

Did you know…?

The brain contains 100 billion neurons. Each neuron can transmit 1,000 nerve impulses per second and make as many as tens of thousands of synaptic contacts.

Every minute, about 750 milliliters of blood, enough to fill a wine bottle, flow through the brain.

The brain can process an image in less than 13 milliseconds – less time than it takes to blink.

The brain is not fully developed until approximately age 25.

The brain has a pattern of connectivity as unique as fingerprints.

It is a myth that we use only 10% of our brains. Brain scans clearly show that we use most of our brain most of the time, even when we're sleeping.

The brain does not have pain receptors or feel pain, but it does *process* pain. Even a brain tumor only causes pain when it has grown large enough to damage bone, blood vessels, or nerves.

We've learned more about the human brain in the last 30 years than we have in all of human history.

The human brain is so amazing, it will blow your mind!

Neuroscience 101 - A Crash Course

I'll be honest; I get a little geeked out over neuroscience. I unabashedly own that. To me, finding a shiny, new nugget of knowledge about the brain is a little like unwrapping a present that I want both to savor and share. The more I learn about how the brain works and the power each of us has to make it work better, the more I want to share it.

I realize that the "Hey, let's grab a glass of wine and talk about the latest neuroscience discovery!" may not the best way to make or keep friends. Let's face it... the very word *neuroscience* can be a bit intimidating to people. But in my conversations, I've found that most people share an innate curiosity about the spongy, three-pound mass of tissue that controls every function of the body from heart rate, immune system, and emotions to our capacity for learning, memory, and creativity.

Since the 1990s, also known as the "Decade of the Brain," knowledge about the human brain has exploded, and many of those discoveries have been made in only the last ten or fifteen years. It is a common misconception that we only use a small percentage of the brain. The human brain is three percent of the body's weight and uses one-fifth of the body's energy. While it's true that at any given moment not all of the regions of the brain may be concurrently firing, we use most of the brain most of the time, even during sleep!

To illustrate, consider what it takes to drink a glass of wine: Reach for the bottle and remove the cork with the corkscrew, pour the wine into a glass, swirl the wine, raise and tilt the glass to observe the legs, breathe in the aroma, and then finally bring the glass to your lips for that first taste. Even if you skipped a step or two, the occipital, frontal, and parietal lobes, sensory motor cortices, and cerebellum are all activated in the time it takes you to open the bottle, pour, and say "Cheers!"

The field of neuroscience is still in its infancy, but this rapid explosion of knowledge has illuminated two significant things: (1) just how misinformed we once were and (2) how much we still have to learn. The scope of the field has grown over the past several decades to include the study of molecular, cellular, developmental, structural, functional, computational, and medical aspects of the nervous system. And yet, even experts will agree that what we don't know about the brain exceeds what we do know. Thanks to technology and advanced research techniques, we've learned more about the human brain in the last 30 years than we have in all of human history!

Whole-Brain Thinking and Learning

Inspired by the misconceptions of left-brain/right-brain research, the construct of "whole-brain thinking" has evolved into a sound framework for learning and cognitive performance. We once believed that people were either "right-brained" or "left-brained." The creative artists, musicians, and poets were right-brained, and the analytical mathematicians, scientists, and engineers were left-brained.

Now we know that this entire theory is an over-simplification. While specific regions of the brain are responsible for specific things, the brain functions as a whole system. The better the regions work independently, the better they integrate with each other. Advances in technology have opened the door to faster and more in-depth research than was possible when the left-brain/right-brain theory was accepted. Back then, the only way to see what was happening in the brain was through invasive procedures primarily performed on people who suffered from mental health problems or neurological diseases.

Today, it is possible to see what happens in a healthy brain when it is exposed to virtually any kind of stimulus while connected to a machine with a few wires and patches. A wealth of research explores how the brain reacts to loud music, soft music, classical music, friendly faces, angry faces, colors, chocolate, alcohol, drugs, and the list goes on and on.

In the world of education, these findings are changing the way educators deliver instruction. The traditional "sit-and-listen" environment has evolved to "maker-spaces" and other more engaging hands-on approaches to learning.

Tremendous academic gains occur when students are exposed to a wide variety of fine and gross motor movement, rich visuals, collaborative projects, and a strong integration of the arts because of the way these experiences engage the whole brain.

Obviously, students have individual learning styles and preferences, which may be right-brain or left-brain dominant. However, when different regions of the brain not normally integrated are engaged, they are able to demonstrate deeper cognition, greater creativity, and improved problem-solving.

The good news is that the benefits of whole-brain thinking and learning are not confined to the classroom. Engaging the whole brain enables learners and thinkers of any age to approach cognitive tasks, creative endeavors, and triggers to stress more efficiently. Generally speaking, all of us have the same pieces and parts in that three-pound squishy mass between our ears. Understanding how it functions, processes data, manages emotions, and enables us to learn, communicate, form memories, and think creatively is the first step in doing all of those things better.

The Neurological Headquarters: Left, Right, Upstairs, Downstairs

Think of the brain in terms of a major organization like Apple. With more than 100,000 employees, the leaders on the executive team all have specific roles and responsibilities to keep the company running. When that team is competent and working together cohesively, the whole organization runs more efficiently.

The brain has a leadership team too, and when they all work together, they enable 100 billion neurons to keep the entire body operating at maximum efficiency. Just as with Apple, when that leadership team effectively manages the individual regions, the mental, physical, emotional, and social functions all contribute to whole-body performance. Think of the "neurological headquarters" as four main regions: left, right, downstairs, and upstairs. It's common knowledge that the brain is split into two hemispheres. Each side is not only anatomically different but is also responsible for very different tasks. The left side of the brain controls the right side of the body. It is logical, linear, and linguistic, and it loves order. Look at all the l-words! Here is where, scientists and mathematicians hang out.

The right side of the brain controls the left side of the body and is creative, intuitive, and emotional. It deals with sensory, experiential feelings, and spatial perceptions. Artists and musicians spend a great deal of time in the right brain. The two hemispheres are connected by a thick band of nerves called the *corpus callosum*. This bridge allows the two hemispheres to communicate.

The essential key to understanding whole-brain thinking is that the brain is designed to work as a system, not as individual parts. We do not function with "half a brain" as the terms left-brained and right-brained imply. It's true that specific regions are primarily responsible for specific brain functions; however, no single region works alone. Instead, all coordinate with one another for data input, processing, and output. For example, a computer programmer may exercise the left side of his brain more than the right side due to the work he does, but that doesn't mean he is left-brained. He uses many regions of the brain to breathe, see, read, write, compute, and more.

Another example is memory. The exact nature of memory is a topic of hot debate, but scientists generally agree that memories are stored at synapses between neurons. As the neurons communicate by sending signals to one another, the connection gets stronger and consequently stitches different aspects of the memory together. That memory may comprise sensory information, emotions, movement, and more, while the hippocampus is primarily responsible for episodic memories. Many parts of the brain contribute to making a specific memory available for recall.

In addition to having two hemispheres, we also have a downstairs brain and an upstairs brain. Some psychologists refer to these as the *feeling brain* and the *thinking brain*. Perhaps a better way to describe them is the *reacting brain* and the *responding brain.* The downstairs brain, or the feeling brain, resides in the space from the bridge of the nose down to the top of the neck. This downstairs brain includes the survival brain and the emotional brain. The survival brain, also called the reptilian brain, involves essential functions like breathing, blinking, instincts, body temperature, heart rate, and other involuntary impulses. The reptilian brain is primitive and only concerned with pain, fear, and danger. Its primary function is to keep us alive.

The emotional brain, or the limbic brain, is wrapped around the reptilian brain and is the reactive part of the brain. We will dig deeper into the limbic system a bit later, but its primary function is to manage emotions and the involuntary mechanisms associated with those emotions.

Strategically placed in the very center of the brain, the amygdala has a critical role in emotional expression. It is the emotional sentinel and has a great deal of power over which regions of the brain are activated. The amygdala responds to a variety of emotional stimuli but most often those related to fear and anxiety.

The upstairs brain, the thinking brain, is much more complex and evolved. The outermost layer of the brain is the cerebral cortex, which is responsible for thinking and processing information from the five senses. Due to the vast knowledge that the human brain accumulates over time, the cerebral cortex undergoes a process called *corticalization*, or wrinkling. This area is one in which we *want* wrinkles. The more we learn, the more wrinkles we have.

The part right behind the forehead is called the *prefrontal cortex*, the location for more sophisticated mental activities such as planning, thinking, and executive functioning. Thanks to a fully developed prefrontal cortex, we are able to distinguish between right and wrong and understand the consequences of our actions. Here, emotional intelligence, empathy, and self-awareness live.

We'd like to believe that the prefrontal cortex, our rational thinking brain, is in charge. In reality, though, it's not even in control most of the time. As sophisticated as it is, it can be "hijacked" by the limbic system. The subconscious brain is the ultimate decision maker, largely because it is responsible for keeping us alive. Who hasn't done something in the heat of anger or when really stressed only to have a "what-was-I-thinking" moment later? When we experience the intense emotions of threat or fear, whether these are real or imagined, the amygdala immediately puts the survival brain on red alert in preparation for fight or flight.

In his 1996 book, *Emotional Intelligence: Why It Can Matter More Than IQ*, Daniel Goleman coined the term *amygdala hijack* to explain how the downstairs brain takes over to survive and puts the upstairs brain, or the thinking brain, on pause. This illustrates the "what-was-I-thinking?" moment when *thinking* is replaced by *reacting*. Neuroscientists have found an inverse relationship between the amygdala and the prefrontal cortex. When the amygdala is active with blood and oxygen, it reduces activation in the prefrontal cortex. When we are really stressed, angry, or upset, the brain sends all the fuel downstairs to the feeling brain and pauses the thinking brain.

For example, imagine walking down a path and suddenly spotting a snake. One's first reaction might be to shriek and jump away. Closer inspection reveals that it isn't a snake after all; it is just a garden hose. The amygdala didn't consult with the prefrontal cortex to determine whether it was a snake or a hose. It automatically sent a first responder to the survival brain to cue a release of adrenalin from the adrenal glands, speed up the heart and breathing rates, send more blood to the muscles, enhance reflexes, and dilate the pupils, all within a fraction of a second! There was no thinking involved. It was all reacting.

One way to prevent an amygdala hijack is to incorporate the practice of mindfulness. MRI scans show that after regular mindfulness practice, the amygdala appears to shrink and the prefrontal cortex becomes thicker and stronger. The neural connectivity in the brain also changes. The connection between the amygdala and the rest of the brain gets weaker, while the networks associated with attention and concentration get stronger. More on how intense emotions and stress create a cascade of responses in the brain and body in greater depth is yet to come.

Lobes of the Brain

When the brain is operating at maximum efficiency, the upstairs and downstairs brains are in constant communication in every brain-related task and function. The survival brain, limbic brain, and the neocortex influence each other, linking emotions to voluntary and involuntary actions. This interplay between the thinking brain and the emotional brain, combined with our experiences and memories, all contribute to our unique personalities.

It is widely accepted that any living thing with a cerebrum has the capacity for conscious thought. The cerebrum is divided into four distinct regions, or lobes, in each hemisphere: the frontal, parietal, occipital, and temporal lobes. Each is made up of two individual lobes. The size and development of the lobes, neural connectivity, social relationships, and a variety of other factors affect the level of consciousness. All of the lobes are either physically connected to one another or connected via nerve signals interacting with each other to process information.

It is a myth that any one brain region is solely responsible for any specific function. Though each lobe has a specific set of functions, many of these functions are inter-dependent with other brain regions. For example, the use of fMRI (functional magnetic resonance imaging) reveals that language-processing activates numerous regions in every major lobe as well as in the cerebellum. Most brain activity requires a coordinated network with the body in response to external stimuli rather than any one region working in isolation.

Frontal lobe
The frontal lobe is made up of two paired lobes known as the left and right frontal cortex. This region is vital to our conscious thought processes and higher-level cognitive functions, and this frontal lobe is in use all the time. It comes into play to decide what to wear or eat as well as when we think about a struggling friend. This lobe enables communication of thoughts fluently and meaningfully. This is where we manage decision-making, problem-solving, and

thinking. Think of the frontal lobe as the executive control center. Our personality, also called the "self-will" area, also lives here as shown when scientists discovered in the mid-1800s that Phineas Gage, a railroad worker, survived a freak accident in which a massive iron post pierced his frontal lobe. While he miraculously survived, his personality changed so drastically that his friends described him as a different person.

Temporal lobe
The temporal lobe consists of a pair of lobes that sit right behind the temples. This lobe is less a separate region and more a home to numerous neural structures such as the limbic system, Wernicke's area, and Broca's area. Here, sensory input, including pain, is processed, and auditory stimuli as well, in order to ensure that a number of unconscious and automatic bodily functions and emotional states, such as sexual arousal and appetite, are engaged.

In addition to processing sound, the temporal lobe enables the comprehension and understanding of language and the retention of visual and emotional memories. In direct communication with the amygdala and hippocampus, it plays vital role in the formation of visual memories, often referred to as the "mind's eye" and the way mental images of people, objects, or places in the past are retrieved.

Like the other lobes, the temporal lobe interacts with information received from various brain regions as well as sensory input from the environment, creating a dynamic and complex mind-body-environment interplay shaped by personal experiences.

Occipital lobe

The occipital lobe is the brain's smallest lobe, but it has the big job of allowing us to see and process external stimuli as well as assign meaning to and remember visual perceptions. Similar to the way the temporal lobe makes sense of auditory information, the occipital lobe processes visual images and links that information with images stored in memory to make sense of what we see. This process includes determining color properties, assessing size and depth, and sending that information to other parts of the brain to assign meaning and determine the appropriate response.

Parietal lobe

The parietal lobe is the brain's primary sensory area where we receive and interpret input from other areas of the body including spatial sense and navigation, touch, temperature, and pain. Some research suggests that the more sensory input a particular body part provides, the more surface area of the parietal lobe is dedicated to that area. For example, because we receive a lot of sensory data from fingers and hands, more of the parietal lobe is dedicated to receiving and processing this input. The parietal lobe is also involved with language processing, number sense, and the manipulation of objects. Although multisensory in nature, scientists call this region the *dorsal stream of vision* referring to the "where" stream (spatial vision) and the "how" stream (vision for acting upon stimuli).

SYNESTHESIA

Some people are born with exceptional senses. And, some people are able to combine senses and experience the world completely differently from the rest of us. The word "synesthesia" is derived from Latin and literally means "concomitant sensations." Synesthetes experience a unique blending of two senses or perceptions. Simply put, when one sense is activated, another unrelated sense is activated at the same time. Synesthetes can taste the sound of thunder, smell the color red, or see the smell of coffee.

Some of the most creative artists, musicians and innovators were synesthetes. Wassily Kandinsky heard hissing sounds when he opened his watercolor paint box as a child. "Lolita" author, Vladimir Nabokov, had grapheme-color synesthesia, which is when people see specific letters in specific colors. "It's called color hearing," Nabokov told the BBC in 1962. "Perhaps one in a thousand has that. But I'm told by psychologists that most children have it, that later they lose that aptitude when they are told by stupid parents that it's all nonsense, an A isn't black, a B isn't brown."

Duke Ellington saw colors and textures in music. He saw a D note as dark blue burlap and a G note as light blue satin. "I hear a note by one of the fellows in the band and it's one color. I hear the same note played by someone else and it's a different color. When I hear sustained musical tones, I see them in textures."

Motor cortex

The motor cortex is located between the frontal lobe and the parietal lobe and spans the top of the brain from ear to ear. This little band works with the cerebellum to coordinate the learning of motor skills.

Limbic system

The limbic system is squished in the center of the brain right above the brain stem. This highly sophisticated part of the brain manages a range of brain functions in various structures such as learning, memory, and emotional processing in the thalamus, hypothalamus, hippocampus, and amygdala as well as the neurotransmitters that affect them.

Because the production of hormones and the way they interact both influence and are influenced by a wide range of internal and external factors, the limbic system is inextricably linked to every part of the body. Stubbing a toe, hearing a sad song, reading a note of appreciation from the boss, hugging a friend, seeing a photograph, kissing a loved one – all of these experiences can trigger limbic reactions that release neurotransmitters.

The limbic system involves a complex range of brain structures, and some scientists identify it as a fifth lobe that includes parts of the other four lobes. In addition, the extent of unconscious reactions that take place in this area has led the way to understanding and treating addiction, OCD, and mental illness. We'll explore the limbic system in further depth a bit later.

Cerebellum

The cerebellum sits right behind the brain stem and comprises only about 10% of the brain's total weight, yet it contains more neurons than the rest of the brain regions combined. The cerebellum monitors all of the impulses sent from the nerves in the muscles and coordinates fine and gross motor movements. It calibrates the detailed form of movements, rather than deciding what movements to execute, such as swinging a golf club or climbing a set of stairs. The cerebellum also stores the memory of specific movements such as tying a shoe or lifting a glass. This is referred to as muscle memory or motor memory.

Corpus Callosum

The corpus callosum is a broad bundle of neural fibers that connect the two hemispheres. It is difficult to talk about whole-brain thinking and learning without giving props to the part of the brain that enables neural communication between the two hemispheres.

Hypothalamus

The hypothalamus is a tiny region about the size of an almond in the center of the brain, which is responsible for a variety of metabolic processes and functions of the autonomic nervous system. One of the most critical functions of the hypothalamus, however, is to link the nervous system with the endocrine system via the pituitary gland. The hypothalamus is responsible for a range of autonomic behaviors such as hunger temperature, and other systems involved in sleep and emotional activity.

The Anatomy of the Brain

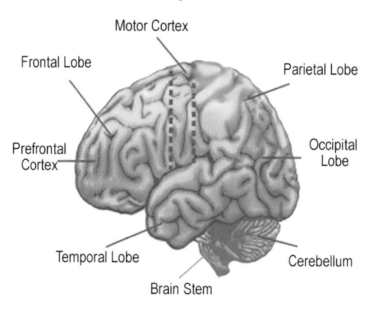

Motor Cortex

Frontal Lobe

Parietal Lobe

Prefrontal Cortex

Occipital Lobe

Temporal Lobe

Cerebellum

Brain Stem

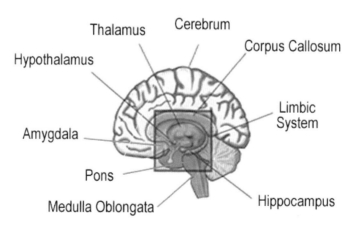

Thalamus

Cerebrum

Hypothalamus

Corpus Callosum

Limbic System

Amygdala

Pons

Medulla Oblongata

Hippocampus

Amygdala

The amygdala is located in the center of the limbic system. It is responsible for the memory of emotions and the body's response to threats and fear, controlling the way we react to any event seen as potentially threatening or dangerous. When the amygdala senses a danger, it releases adrenalin and starts a chain reaction of changes in preparation for fight or flight. These include an increase in heart and breathing rates, an increase in blood to the muscles, and enhanced reflexes. In extremely stressful or frightening situations, people are also desensitized to pain so that all resources are devoted to the danger.

Hippocampus

Humans and other mammals have two hippocampi, one in each temporal lobe. Uniquely shaped like a seahorse, it is responsible for episodic memory, spatial cognition, and response inhibition – the ability to override a natural or dominant behavioral response to a stimulus for a more-appropriate or goal-oriented behavior.

Thalamus

The thalamus is located just below the corpus callosum and acts as a relay station. Every sensory system, except smell, is received by the thalamus and relayed to the appropriate region of the brain for processing. The thalamus also plays a vital role in regulating sleep and consciousness. Degeneration of the thalamus can cause an inability to sleep or a state of total insomnia which can lead to death. Damage to this region can lead to a permanent coma.

Pons

The pons is part of the brainstem that includes neural pathways and tracts that conduct signals from the cerebral cortex to the cerebellum as well as tracts that carry the sensory signals to the thalamus. It also plays a crucial role in REM sleep, or the state in which we experience dreams.

Medulla oblongata

The medulla oblongata could easily be thought of as the body's MVP. Every involuntary function performed here regulates life-sustaining functions such as blood pressure, breathing, and swallowing as well as the transfer of neural messages from the brain to the spinal cord and body.

Putting it All Together

The prefrontal cortex is responsible for executive functions, but it works much more efficiently when the rest of the team shows up to help. Imagine brainstorming creative ideas for a new product launch. The prefrontal cortex is in charge of generating all of the ideas for messaging, the vision for graphics, and go-to-market strategy; however, whole-brain thinkers will invite the temporal lobe to the table, perhaps with a little soft background music by Claude Debussy. The specialized skills of the temporal lobe will enable the prefrontal cortex to tap into the unconscious where the creative impulses live. It is also known that jazz and "new age" music with no dominant rhythm (or linear melody line) can promote a sense of relaxed alertness that helps inspire creativity, generate new ideas, and precipitate "flow mode." Also known as being "in the zone," scientists believe this is the key to productivity and creativity.

Psychologist Mihàly Csìkszentmihàlyi coined the term flow mode in his quest to find out "what makes life worth living." He discovered that pleasure and lasting satisfaction can be found in activities that bring about a state of flow – the optimal state of consciousness where we feel and perform at our best.

He studied thousands of people, from sculptors to CEOs to factory workers, and asked them to record their feelings at intervals throughout the working day. Csìkszentmihàlyi observed that when people were fully immersed in an activity or challenge they became so laser-focused on the task that all other noise and distractions faded away.

"With other colleagues around the world, we have done over 8,000 interviews of people – from Dominican monks, to blind nuns, to Himalayan climbers, to Navajo shepherds – who enjoy their work. And regardless of the culture, regardless of education or whatever, there are these seven conditions that seem to be there when a person is in flow. There's this focus that, once it becomes intense, leads to a sense of ecstasy, a sense of clarity: you know exactly what you want to do from one moment to the other; you get immediate feedback. You know that what you need to do is possible to do, even though difficult, and sense of time disappears, you forget yourself, you feel part of something larger. And once the conditions are present, what you are doing becomes worth doing for its own sake.

- Mihàly Csìkszentmihàlyi, TED2004

When we enter flow mode, the brain transitions from the fast-moving beta brainwaves of waking consciousness to the borderline state between alpha waves, which are often associated with daydreaming, and theta waves that typically only occur during REM sleep. In addition, flow is the result of *transient hypofrontality*, the deactivation of our sense of self. When the dorsolateral prefrontal cortex is paused, the inner critic, that voice of doubt and insecurity is quieted. As a result, we're far more courageous, imaginative, and open to seeing new possibilities.

The limbic system also releases large quantities of pleasure-inducing chemicals such as dopamine, serotonin, endorphins and norepinephrine that amp up focus and creativity. This performance-enhancing cocktail is also responsible for lowering signal-to-noise ratios, thus increasing the ability to identify patterns and link ideas together in new ways. These changes in chemistry and brain waves have opened to door to a wealth of research exploring the impact of flow on productivity, creativity and happiness.

A 10-year study conducted by McKinsey found that top executives were five times more productive when working in the flow state. Other studies indicate significant correlations between flow states and higher learning attitudes and outcomes. Maybe the most important finding that came out of Csìkszentmihàlyi's work, one of the largest psychological studies ever conducted, was that the people who have the most flow in their lives are the happiest people on Earth.

THE POWER OF FLOW MODE

Musicians who create rap have also contributed to a deeper understanding of the neurological phenomenon known as flow state. Neuroscientists at the National Institute on Deafness and Communication Disorders examined the brains of 12 professional rappers using an fMRI scanner. They played an instrumental track and first asked the artists to rap memorized lyrics. Then they asked them to freestyle – improvise and create lyrics on the spot. Researchers identified huge differences in their brain activity between the memorized and the freestyle lyrics.

Brain scans showed that when the rappers were engaged in freestyle lyrics, the dorsolateral prefrontal cortex was temporarily deactivated enabling them to enter a state of flow. Researchers discovered an entire, unique network of neural connectivity in regions of the brain that manage language, emotion, motor function, and sensory processing during freestyle rapping.

Harvard's Teresa Amiable discovered that not only are people more creative in flow, they also report being more creative the day after a flow state. This finding suggests that flow can actually train us to be more creative over time, not just in the moment. Other research maintains that the ability to enter flow mode is a key component to happiness.

"One thing I have learned in a long life: That all our science, measured against reality, is primitive and childlike — and yet it is the most precious thing we have."

The Limbic System: The Brain's Pharmacy

The limbic system is the emotional center of the brain where we manage happiness, sadness, fear, anger, empathy, and other emotions. Emotion plays an enormous role in the brain's capacity to learn and function properly. The stronger the emotions are toward a specific event or experience, the stronger the limbic system responds either to impede or to enhance cognition and file that experience away in long-term memory.

Located just beneath the cerebral cortex, the limbic system is directly responsible for releasing chemicals called neurotransmitters in response to certain emotions. The particular emotion felt determines which neuro-transmitter the limbic system produces. Cortisol and adrenalin, for example, are released in response to intense fear, anger, or stress as part of the brain's fight-or-flight mechanism.

The brain produces other chemicals like serotonin, oxytocin, and endorphins when positive emotions like pleasure, happiness, and love are felt. Others such as dopamine, glutamate, and GABA (an amino acid that acts as a neurotransmitter by inhibiting nerve transmission) play essential roles in cognition and brain circuitry.

These neurotransmitters help regulate mood and emotions and have an enormous impact on performance and overall well-being. In addition, they play a significant role in cognition, memory, and resilience. Put simply, they can significantly impede or enhance executive function, self-regulation, memory, and creativity.

As neurotransmitters help us regulate our emotions, they also serve as the on/off switch for cognition and learning. If the limbic system is fighting stress, it stops everything else to conquer the threat, and that is exactly how it is supposed to work. Remember the amygdala hijack? Chemicals are released in response to the emotion and a host of changes happen automatically. Blood-pressure and blood-sugar levels increase to create a boost of energy. Heart rate and breathing also increase, circulating the cortisol throughout the whole body.

The intensity of the emotion brought on by the stimulus determines the magnitude of the physiological response. Common stressors such as a demanding boss or coworker, financial constraints, or even just being stuck in traffic can hijack the amygdala, and release chemicals that engage the survival brain and put the rational thinking brain on lockdown. The limbic system is a busy place. Every emotional response results in the release of chemicals activating various parts of the brain and body.

Neurotransmitters – The Short List

To date, neuroscientists have identified over 60 different neurotransmitters and continue to study the roles they play in cognition, behavior, learning, emotions, communication, and even sleep patterns. While they are often classified as having a single or primary function, new research indicates they are multi-faceted, and their interactions can be highly complex. For example, dopamine is frequently called the "pleasure and reward chemical;" however, neuroscientists have found that acetylcholine is a neurotransmitter that stimulates the production of dopamine, and the combination of the two chemicals significantly enhances cognition.

The following list explains a few of the more common neurotransmitters that play a significant role in memory, learning, social interaction, mental health, and overall well-being, all of which will be explored in more detail in the coming chapters. This section will provide a top-line explanation of the primary chemicals and how they affect us.

Dopamine: reward and pleasure

Dopamine is the "I-did-it!" drug, one which helps regulate the reward and pleasure center. Not only does it allow us to enjoy certain rewards, but it also motivates us towards the experience. A dopamine rush comes after earning a promotion, working hard on a project, losing 10 pounds after sticking to a diet, or finally finishing that 5K race.

People who demonstrate little drive, initiative, enthusiasm or self-confidence may suffer from low levels of dopamine. Studies compared dopamine levels between rats that had two options to get food, an easy task for minimal food and a harder one that produced twice as much food. Those with low dopamine levels chose the easy task for the minimum amount of food. Conversely, the rats with high dopamine levels worked harder to get more food.

People who suffer from addiction may be overproducing dopamine. Because the reward circuit in the brain also includes areas involved with motivation, memory, and pleasure, remembering how good something felt – the high, the rush, the buzz – floods the brain with dopamine and hijacks the prefrontal cortex to go after the source of the pleasure. Over time, consistently high levels of dopamine physically change the brain by desensitizing neurons, accounting for why some people eventually need more to get the same "buzz."

Serotonin: mood and well-being

Serotonin, also called the "calming chemical," is primarily responsible for managing mood, anxiety, and happiness, and also for rewarding social behavior. The brain produces it when we feel significant, respected, or important. Recognition from a colleague or family member for doing a good deed or making a major contribution can produce a boost. Exposure to the sunshine, even if only for a few minutes, can also stimulate a release of serotonin.

Low levels of serotonin are associated with depression,

although it has yet to be proven whether a decrease in serotonin causes depression or depression causes a decrease in serotonin. A lack of serotonin also impacts appetite regulation, sleep, memory, and decision-making behaviors. Someone with a bad case of the blues is likely to find that an increase in serotonin will make a difference.

Oxytocin: trust and belonging

Also known as the "hug drug" or "cuddle chemical," oxytocin is the chemical produced when we experience the human connection, trust, and sexual arousal. Oxytocin naturally surges during childbirth, breastfeeding, laughter, and orgasm. But giving someone a hug or demonstrating simple random acts of kindness will also result in an oxytocin surge.

Low levels of oxytocin have been linked to depression, autism, and a range of anxiety disorders. Oxytocin and cortisol are on opposite ends of the hormonal seesaw. As the production of cortisol goes up, it forces the production of oxytocin to go down and vice versa.

Studies have shown that interpersonal touching such as hugging and kissing raises oxytocin levels and decreases cardiovascular stress. Oxytocin is now being tested as a treatment for schizophrenia and autism as well as a potential anti-addictive hormone. Despite the fact that it was discovered in 1952 and listed on the World Health Organization's List of Essential Medicines, neuroscientists agree that much remains to be learned about oxytocin.

Endorphins: pain relief and happiness

Endorphins are commonly known as the chemicals released in response to pain, fear, or stress. Sex, intense exercise, and even some foods like hot peppers (which contain capsaicin) can all generate the feelings of euphoria with an endorphin rush. They are typically produced as a response to fear or pain and are found in the regions of the brain responsible for blocking pain. Interestingly, the brain does not have pain receptors, so it does not actually feel pain; however, the brain is the pain processing center for the entire body.

There are over 20 different kinds of endorphins with some proven to be as potent as morphine and codeine in our pain-management pharmacy. Endorphins can also trigger heightened rage and anxiety. If the hypothalamus doesn't receive the endorphins accurately, it will open the cortisol floodgates at the smallest indication of trouble.

Glutamate: facilitates neural communication

Glutamate is the most prominent neurotransmitter in the body, present in over 50% of the nervous tissue, and it is the brain's primary excitatory neurotransmitter by increasing the electrochemical transmissions of information. Healthy glutamate production contributes to the molecular processes in the hippocampus and cortex, regions that play a significant role in learning and memory.

An excess of glutamate can overstimulate the brain and result in *excitotoxicity*, a term that literally means "exciting neurons to death." Excitotoxicity has been linked to strokes, seizures, traumatic brain injuries, and other chronic diseases like Alzheimer's and Lou Gehrig's disease.

GABA (Gamma-Aminobutyric Acid): inhibits neural communication

GABA is made from glutamate for the purpose of naturally counteracting its excitatory effects. This amino acid acts as a neurotransmitter by inhibiting nerve transmissions when they become overexcited. While glutamate facilitates nerve impulses, GABA works to prevent them from firing. Without GABA, nerve cells fire too often, creating the conditions for panic attacks, seizures, and other anxiety disorders. Glutamate is a double espresso, and GABA is more like warm milk.

Cortisol, adrenaline, and norepinephrine: stress

Cortisol, adrenaline, and norepinephrine are the three major stress hormones. Adrenaline is the "fight, flight, or freeze" hormone and is produced by the adrenal glands when the brain signals danger. It is responsible for the body's immediate physical reactions to a stressful situation such as an increase in heart rate or a surge of energy.

Norepinephrine is the arousal hormone produced in the adrenal glands and the brain and is the hormone that increases awareness and focus. It also reallocates the blood flow away from areas like the skin and shifts it toward more essential areas like the heart and muscles.

Cortisol is the stress hormone. While adrenaline and

norepinephrine are produced in seconds, the release of cortisol can take up to a few minutes. Producing cortisol involves a multi-step process involving two other hormones as well as activity in the hypothalamus, the pituitary gland, and the adrenal glands.

Long-term stress and elevated stress-hormone levels are linked to insomnia, chronic fatigue syndrome, thyroid disorders, dementia, depression, and other conditions. People who are unable to produce healthy amounts of cortisol may suffer from adrenal fatigue, low thyroid function, low blood pressure, blood-sugar imbalances, and lowered immune function.

Acetylcholine: neuroplasticity, movement, and learning
Acetylcholine was the very first neurotransmitter to be identified. It is primarily responsible for activating voluntary muscle movement by translating intention into action between the neuron and the muscle fibers. Too much acetylcholine is associated with depression, while too little can precipitate dementia. An imbalance of this chemical can have physical effects ranging from convulsions to paralysis.

THE SCIENCE OF CRYING

Why do we cry? Charles Darwin declared emotional tears "purposeless." Almost two centuries later, emotional crying is still somewhat of a mystery. We produce three types of tears: basal, reflex, and psychic. Basal and reflex tears have the physiological purpose of lubricating the eye and flushing out foreign particles. While other species shed tears as a result of pain or irritation, humans are the only creatures who shed psychic tears - tears triggered by emotions. New evidence suggests that crying is more than a demonstration of sadness; it's a way to trigger human connection. Crying is a visible signal to others that there is a problem beyond one's ability to cope.

A 2016 study published in Motivation and Emotion showed that tears activate compassion in a way that other expressions of distress do not. When subjects were shown photographs of people crying compared to the same photographs with the tears digitally removed, they reported feeling more connected to those with tears and had a stronger urge to reach out to offer consolation in some way. Neuroscientists have discovered that the same neuronal areas are activated by seeing someone cry as crying oneself. Michael Trimble, behavioral neurologist and the leading expert on crying explained, "There must have been some point in time, evolutionarily, when the tear became something that automatically set off empathy and compassion in one another. Being able to cry emotionally and being able to respond to that is a very important part of being human."

Mental States Create Neural Traits

Emotional experiences such as happiness, worry, love, and stress create synapses, which, in turn, create an imprint in the neural structure. The longer the focus on the experience, the more intense it is, or the more it is repeated, the more likely that mental state will become an imprinted neural trait. If a person is in a bad psychological state day after day, this negative state will eventually become a characteristic of that person's personality or neural trait.

Such a result is due, in part, to the constant flow of cortisol produced by the negative emotions but may also perpetuated by the negative feedback loop called the vicious cycle. When the brain is focused on adverse events, it gets stuck in a feedback loop that causes it to continue to look for adverse events.

We've all had those days when nothing seems to go right. Even though there may not actually be more bad things on that particular day, the brain may just be more tuned in to the negatives. The more focus on the negatives, the more the brain creates neural pathways designed to deal with them by producing the neurotransmitters that stop productive brain function to address the stress. Because the brain is wired to deal with the negative things, it notices these more. On the other hand, the more the focus is on the positives, the more the brain will accommodate, allowing the positives to produce those good chemicals that create optimum conditions for cognitive function.

The happier you are, the more you'll see the good things. The more good things you see, the more you'll fuel your happiness.

While some people experience more tragedy, loss, or disappointment than others, the real difference between the pessimist and the optimist lies in brain chemistry. The real obstacle to positivity is that our brains are hard-wired for negativity. What has enabled our species to survive as hunters and gatherers is being aware of threats and dangers right around every corner. Today, we aren't faced with the threat of being eaten by a bear, but that survival mechanism still exists to keep us safe. When the threat is real, it's a good thing. But when the threat is imagined or exaggerated, it influences mental and physical health.

Dr. Martin Seligman is known as the Father of Positive Psychology and the leading expert on how optimism and pessimism impact resiliency, cognitive function and health. In his book, *Learned Optimism*, Seligman states that changing how we think changes how we feel, and we have the ability to choose the way we think. Seligman has found one very important distinction between optimists and pessimist. Pessimists attribute failures and obstacles to factors beyond their control while optimists see them as learning experiences and opportunities for growth. We'll learn more about optimism and Dr. Seligman's work a bit later.

4 Ways to Nurture Your Inner Optimist

Research shows that only 10% of long-term happiness is attributed to factors beyond our control.   According to positive psychologists, we have the ability to rewire the brain for greater optimism by developing some very simple habits. Here are four scientifically proven ways to do that.

1. Keep a gratitude journal. The brain reacts the same to real experiences and imagined experiences. Journaling about positive experiences and people who enrich your life lets your brain re-experience them releases the good stress-relieving chemicals all over again.
2. Exercise daily. Physical activity releases stress in the body and good chemicals in the brain. Exercising outside gives you an added bonus of the benefits of nature.
3. Perform random acts of kindness. Write a positive email to someone who is important to you or help another person with no expectation of a return.
4. Engage in flow experiences. Any activity you enjoy and that fully engages your senses can enable you to experience flow state.

THE SCIENCE OF GRUDGES

Humans are masters of resentment and, despite the importance of letting go, we love to hold a grudge. Like other emotions, the capacity for hate and resentment are learned, but they are wired into our DNA. Holding a grudge is really an evolved mental state rooted in desire of a particular outcome. We get deep satisfaction from knowing that those who have harmed us have realized they wronged us.

In neurological terms, it involves the behavioral activation system, the release of dopamine and the prefrontal cortex. Michael McCullough, a professor of psychology at the University of Miami, maintains that resentments and grudges are directly related to goal-seeking and the desire to satiate a craving.

"This ancient brain system seems to produce this craving, and the sense that fulfillment is just around the corner," said McCullough. "It's not the seeking of pleasure or the reward itself, but rather the desire to move towards that goal It's the sense of unease that gives the desire for revenge its compulsive quality."

McCullough found that people holding grudges generate an increase in cortisol and that cortisol levels linked to an interpersonal conflict decrease when we make conciliatory gestures toward people who hurt us. Finding forgiveness and making amends do not just bring us peace; they actually change the circuitry of the brain.

"The mind that opens to a new idea never returns to its original size."

Growing the Capacity to Learn

Is it possible that everything we've learned about learning is wrong? Okay... maybe not everything, but people are much smarter about learning how the brain learns than in times past. Belief once was that intelligence and creativity were fixed, and that people did the best they could with what they had. Today, research shows that the brain is more like Play-Doh than plaster. It is malleable and changes throughout our lives.

Since the 1990s, also known as "the Decade of the Brain," it has been proven that creativity, innovation, critical thinking, and problem-solving are hardwired within each of us, thus increasing the capacity for all of these cognitive processes. The capacity to grow new cells and to make new neural connections comes into play as new things are learned, and unused cells removed, or killed, through stress. The brain also changes chemically and structurally from intense, repeated, or prolonged experiences. All of these processes are *neurogenesis* and *neuroplasticity* at work and explain why each of us can be smarter today than we were yesterday.

Neurogenesis

Anyone who knows the difference between the Charlie Brown Christmas tree and the Rockefeller Center tree is halfway to a basic understanding of neurogenesis. The term *neurogenesis* is made up of the word parts *neuro,* meaning *relating to nerves,* and *genesis,* meaning *the formation* or *creation.* Neurogenesis just means the formation and development of neurons.

The human brain has more than 100 billion neurons, a neuron being the basic working unit of the brain designed to transmit information electrochemically. Brain neurons form about four weeks after conception, and as the fetus continues to grow and experience stimuli, the neurons produce dendrites and axons. The axons send electro-chemical signals, and the dendrites receive them through small gaps called *synapses.*

Neural growth in the womb is extraordinary, at a rate of 250,000 neurons per minute, and they all work overtime to create the dendrites, synapses, and axons necessary to communicate with one another. This process is called *dendritic branching* and is the foundation for all brain activity. At birth, the number of synapses per neuron is 2,500. By age 2, that number increases to more than 15,000 per neuron.

This proliferation of neuron growth is called *transient exuberance* because it is only temporary. The brain's natural pruning process kicks in to clean up and organize all of those unused, malformed, or misconnected dendrites. This process of growing and pruning continues throughout our lives, but those first few years set the stage for neural growth and cognitive function.

After that first major pruning, our dendritic branches look like the Charlie Brown Christmas tree; however, between the ages of three and twelve, dendrites grow at an astonishing rate. Think about how a toddler begins to explore the world. Everything he sees and experiences is a discovery. The more the child experiences as he learns sounds, shapes, colors, safety, fear, love, and a multitude of other things, the more dendrites he grows.

Even as adults, every time we learn something new, dendrites grow as does the capacity for them to communicate, increasing the ability to learn more. In time, all of that growing and learning and pruning enables the Charlie Brown Christmas tree to grow into the Rockefeller Center tree.

Neuroplasticity

It is no secret that the more a person does something, the better that person will be at it. To get better at foul shots, shoot more foul shots. To become better at speaking French, speak more French. Scientifically speaking, neurons that fire together wire together. Right now, some of the 100 billion neurons are busy transmitting signals in your brain via synapses just to read this page. The busiest regions of the brain need more oxygen and glucose to make sense of the letters and words you see so they receive more blood to facilitate the activity.

The occipital lobe takes the printed words and sends different information to other parts of the brain for processing. The temporal lobe decodes the words and uses phonological awareness to recognize them. The frontal lobe enables comprehension of the meaning of the words and sentences. The parietal lobe acts as a conductor coordinating all of the electrical impulses and linking the brain regions together, so they can work in concert. The more energy those regions of the brain have, the more synapses they can create. And the more active all of those regions are over time, the stronger the neural connections become and the better they function.

Because the brain is a learning muscle, intense, prolonged, or repeated experiences change its structure and chemistry. Neuroscientists refer to this as *experience-dependent neuroplasticity*. The more a specific region of the brain is used, the stronger that region becomes. For example, studies show that taxi drivers in London have developed thicker neural layers in their hippocampus, the part of the brain that helps with visual-spatial memories.

The London taxi cab driver is as famous as the black cab he drives because he is required to know immediately the quickest route to any destination without the aid of a map or GPS. The streets of London are extremely complex and were not constructed in typical vertical and horizontal grid patterns. To be licensed, London taxi drivers must pass a test called "The Knowledge." Those who pass this test are described as having the streets of London imprinted on their brains.

The Black Cab driver also has a larger hippocampus than most people. The hippocampus is responsible for short-term memory, long-term memory and spatial memory, all of which enable navigation. Because taxi drivers use this part of the brain day in and day out, that brain is physically changed and grown over time.

Learning is not just about building neural connections; it is also about getting rid of old ones. Such a process is called "synaptic pruning," and the "use-it-or-lose-it" principle applies here. Think back to studying for a high school history test covering the Reconstruction, the election of 1876, and the 14th Amendment. If none of that sounds at all familiar, just know that these topics were real lessons. No doubt the material was covered in the textbook several times and also explained by the teacher. Read, reread, outline, highlight, rinse and repeat. That whole process created new neural pathways to sear the information to memory.

Okay, now... years later, how many of us remember anything about the Reconstruction? What happened to those neural circuits built during test preparation? Unless you're a history buff or simply enjoy impressing friends with 1876 trivia, most likely most or all of that knowledge is lost because it hasn't been used. Just as with any other muscle, the brain atrophies without exercise. Neural connections are no longer engaged as they get pruned away; if nurtured, however, these connections continue to grow and connect with other neural circuits. Educators refer to this as *building on prior knowledge* and *scaffolding*. From a neurological perspective, this process connects ideas and bridges knowledge gaps.

Think of it as akin to growing a vegetable garden. Once seeds are planted in fertile soil and treated to time with sunlight and water, the seeds grow roots; those roots grow stems, leaves and flowers; and those flowers grow into vegetables. Watchful tending of the garden eliminates critters, pests, and weeds. The more the plants are nurtured, the bigger and stronger they grow.

Like those seedlings in the garden, everything learned starts out as dendrites that grow out of neurons and connect with other neurons. The more information is used, added to, reflected on, and applied, the bigger and stronger that neural circuit grows. The limbic system produces good chemicals that travel along these connections, fertilizing them like Miracle-Gro®. Other chemicals, like the cortisol produced with stress, break the circuits down and kill them just as Roundup® does in the garden.

Glial cells, or astrocytes, are another type of brain cell that plays an important role in cognition. Little was known about glial cells until the 1980s when Dr. Marian Diamond discovered that Albert Einstein had more of them than the

SELLING TO INSOMNIACS

If you've ever suffered from insomnia, then you've probably seen those gimmicky infomercials featuring bad actors over-dramatizing some mild inconvenience until they discover the life-changing inventions like the Potty Putter to improve putting while on the toilet, or the Hawaii Chair to build rock-hard abs doing the hula at your desk. (I promise I did not make these up. Google them... you'll see for yourself.)

It would be logical to assume that these cheesy infomercials were on late at night because those were the cheapest time slots. As it turns out, the ads are more effective in the middle of the night than during the day. So, what makes the graveyard timeslot work? Two neurological factors are at work. First, people who are watching paid programming in the middle of the night are not sleeping which means their glial cells are not working flushing out neurotoxins and dead cells. All of this clutters the brain and prevents new and stronger neural connections from growing. In addition, mental fatigue undermines rational decision making and defaults to emotionally based choices.

But wait... there's more! Even if you don't "ACT NOW" to score a second Potty Putter or Hawaii Chair for additional shipping and handling, the product is planted in your head. If you see it again on television or the "As Seen on TV" shelves at the store, it's more familiar and that familiarity makes it more appealing. You may suddenly realize how much you need it.

average person. *Glia* comes from the Greek word for *glue*, and it was assumed that they were just that: brain glue that supported the neurons. It is now known that these cells are essential for brain development and function, perhaps even for intelligence.

Glial cells have a full-time job, working during the day to facilitate neural connectivity and communication. As they do, they are also on the lookout for circuits that aren't pulling their weight. When they see an unused connection, like the 1876 election, they mark it with a protein. The glial cells on night shift look for the circuits marked with proteins as well as neurotoxins and cells killed with cortisol. Their job is to sweep all of that debris away; however, they can only do that during sleep when neural cells shrink to make the interstitial spaces larger, thus giving the glial cells room to work and flush everything out.

When sleep is interrupted, the glial cells cannot do their job. The neurotoxins and dead cells clutter the brain, and the unused connections prevent new and stronger connections from growing, similar to neglecting a flower garden and letting the weeds take over, eventually choking out the flowers. In addition, mental fatigue undermines rational decision-making and defaults to emotionally based choices.

THE PARADOX OF HAPPINESS

No one likes to be cranky or in a bad mood. However, new research reveals that those negative moods have their perks and chasing happiness has a downside. Negative moods summon a more attentive, skeptical thinking style that leads to critical examination. When we feel happy and carefree, we tend to look for easy answers, avoid challenges, and jump to conclusions.

Striving for happiness can also have a paradoxical effect. In one study, participants were given a fictitious article that praised the benefits of happiness while the control group read an article that made no mention of happiness. Both groups then watched a series of film clips, and participants were asked to rate their level of happiness after each clip. The group primed with the happiness article reported feeling less happy than those in the control group. Placing greater emphasis on the importance of finding happiness increased their expectations for how things should be.

Psychologists have discovered that the quest for happiness is fundamentally incompatible with the very essence of happiness. Those who crusade to find it create expectations of others that inevitably lead to resentments and disappointment. Real happiness comes from interacting with people or engaging in activities you genuinely enjoy rather than to fulfill the desire to make yourself happy.

"The most beautiful experience we can have is the mysterious. It is the fundamental emotion that stands at the cradle of true art and true science."

The Gray Matters of Pray Matters

What started out as an ordinary day for a man named Saul back in A.D. 36 turned out to be one of monumental significance for civilizations to come. According to the story recounted in the book of Acts, Saul was on his way to Damascus to murder the disciples when he fell to the ground blinded by a flash of light. The accompanying voice of Jesus Christ told him to continue on his journey where he would meet Ananias who would restore his sight. He then became baptized, changed his name to Paul, and the entire religious experience transformed him into a believer and evangelist.

While biblical scholars have long accepted the conversion of Saul to Paul as proof of the power of God, neuroscientists have been exploring a scientific explanation. One theory is that Saul/Paul suffered from a neurological disorder. The fall to the ground, the flash of light, and the voice from above were all symptoms of an epileptic seizure in the temporal lobe, and the temporary blindness was a result of an altered state of conscientious that often follows such a seizure.

The relationship between epilepsy and religiosity has been explored at length. Vilayanur Ramachandran, author of *Phantoms in the Brain* and *The Tell-Tale Brain*, was included in TIME Magazine's 2011 most 100 influential people in the world for his work focused on "changing how our brains think about our minds." He was also the first clinical researcher to link the temporal lobes with religious sensations at the University of California in San Diego back in the late 1990s.

Ramachandran examined patients suffering from an unusual form of epilepsy and concluded that the brain's temporal lobe – which the scientists dubbed the "God module" – may affect how intensely a person responds to religious experiences. Ramachandran's team compared temporal-lobe epilepsy patients with healthy controls as they tested their involuntary physical responses to stimuli by measuring the electrical conductivity of their skin. Three groups of words were presented to the subjects: neutral words, sexual words, and religious words. The control group responded most intensely to the sexual words while showing no significant response to the neutral or religious words. The subjects with temporal lobe epilepsy generated the most significant reaction from the religious words while sexual words generated less of a response than neutral ones. Ramachandran maintains that his work was never intended to validate or invalidate the existence of God, but instead to explore the way the brain processes spiritual experiences and determine whether some people are more neurologically predisposed to religion than others.

If the abnormal brain activity of epilepsy patients alters one's response to religious concepts, could changing one's brain patterns artificially do the same for people without epilepsy? This is the question that Michael Persinger set out to explore in a study conducted at Laurentian University in Ontario. Dr. Persinger's famous "God helmet" was designed to stimulate activity in the temporal lobes and artificially create a religious experience.

Participants reported seeing "presences" to be that of angels, the deceased known to the subjects, and other mystical beings. Some of the subjects even reported experiencing what they perceived to be God. Persinger maintained that 80% of his subjects reported "feeling the presence of a spirit" or having a "profound feeling of cosmic bliss" when wearing the helmet. However, his research was scientifically scrutinized as "technically flawed" when it was unable to be replicated and when Britain's most renowned atheist, Richard Dawkins, did not experience God, merely dizziness and tingling in his limbs.

Despite a wealth of research connecting temporal lobe epilepsy and spiritual experiences, it turns out that our gray matters and our pray matters are far more complex than a single region of the brain. Some people are so deeply religious that scientists concede to the difficulty of extrapolating religious beliefs from other cognitive thought processes. It is, however, reasonable to assume that there may be neurological processes at work in believers' brains that are absent in nonbelievers' brains.

Recent imaging studies have shown that religiosity activates an elaborate neural network integrating the frontal, parietal and temporal lobes. Beyond neural activity, the controversial research of whether the brain is "hardwired" for religion has spawned a new discipline called *neurotheology* to investigate the neural correlates of religious and spiritual beliefs to determine why some people are more inclined towards spirituality, while others remain deeply skeptical about of God's existence.

Some neurotheologians argue that the brain – specifically the limbic system – is emotionally wired for a predisposition to believe in God while others suggest that religious ideology is embedded in our genes. Numerous studies indicate that religious and spiritual experiences activate the brain reward circuits in much the same way as love, sex, gambling, drugs and music.

One segment of the research community maintains that religious belief is a side effect in the human quest for understanding and that belief in a higher spiritual power is just a manifestation of a biological phenomenon that makes the human brain so intelligent and adaptable. Still, others say that while the research may be able to identify electrical impulses and brain activation of religious experience and practice, belief in God is a combination of nurture and nature and far more than the sum of its experiences.

Dean Hamer, PhD, a behavioral geneticist who has worked at the National Cancer Institute (NCI) and the NIH, compared more than 2,000 DNA samples and concluded that spirituality is a genetic phenomenon that can be described and measured while religion is the cultural counterpart – the ideas, values, and rituals passed down from one generation to another. Hamer believes religion is rooted in nurture and spirituality is rooted in nature.

Hamer asked participants more than 200 questions to determine their level of spirituality. He found that the higher their score, the greater the person's ability to believe in a spiritual force, and the more likely they were to have the VMAT2 gene. According to Hamer, the "God gene" is a genetic predisposition to certain qualities that enable one to be more spiritual. He identified three qualities as possible predispositions in correlation with this gene: "self-forgetfulness" (the ability to become completely absorbed in something), "transpersonal identification" (the ability to feel connected to something larger than yourself), and "mysticism" (the ability to believe in things that are unprovable).

Andrew Newberg, a pioneer in neurotheology and author of the books *"Principles of Neuro-theology"* and *"How God Changes Your Brain"* has observed that religious thoughts are not invisible using single photon emission computed tomography technology to measure blood flow in the brain. When people are engaged in religious practices, multiple lobes of their brain work together to create a powerful emotional experience. By injecting radioactive tracers into Buddhist, Michael Baime's bloodstream, Newberg could see precisely what was happening in his brain at the height of a meditative trance. Brain scans showed that the temporal lobes were engaged, but of even greater interest was the fact that the parietal lobes appeared to shut down almost completely. The parietal lobes give us our sense of time and place. Without them, we lose our "sense of self" and instead experience a sense of personal insignificance that leads to a feeling of oneness with God.

Newberg's work suggests a greater emotional significance of religion. Newberg explained, "People don't feel that they're purposely making it happen. They feel that they are being basically overcome by the experience. For them, it's the spirit of God which is moving through them. I can't prove that or disprove that on the basis of a brain scan, but I can see the changes that are going on in the brain while they're engaged in this very, very powerful and very deep spiritual practice... It certainly looks like the way the brain is put together makes it very easy for human beings to have religious and spiritual experiences."

Newberg also points to neuroplasticity as an explanation. Brain scans of highly religious people who engage in meditation and meditative prayers or mantras (such as prayer that repeats a particular phrase) show more activity in frontal-lobe areas such as the prefrontal cortex, compared with people who were not long-term meditators. Strengthening these areas of the brain may help people to be calmer and less reactionary when faced with stressors. Newberg also suggests that the beliefs and teachings advocated by religion become integrated into one's neural connections. The more that specific neural connections in the brain are used, the stronger they become. If a particular religion advocates compassion or forgiveness, the neural circuits involved in thinking about compassion and forgiveness become stronger.

Others argue that belief in God is influenced by cognitive style. Studies conducted by Amitai Shenhav and his colleagues at Harvard University in 2011 support their hypothesis that religiosity is determined by one's tendency to rely on intuition over reflection. Participants completed the Cognitive Reflection Test, an assessment comprised of math problems that, although easily solvable, have intuitively compelling incorrect answers. Participants who gave more intuitive answers on the test reported having a stronger belief in God. This effect held firm despite controls for education level, income, political orientation, or other demographic variables. Another study showed that the correlation between CRT scores and belief in God also exists when controlled for intelligence (IQ) and personality differences.

Biologist, Lionel Tiger of Rutgers University, maintains that religious belief is rooted in an evolutionary drive for the release of serotonin. Tiger concludes that the neurochemical response of religious experiences serves a biological need for the feeling of well-being. He points to France as evidence – a predominantly Catholic country with low attendance at church and Europe's highest consumption of antidepressants. Attending a religious service or participation in religious rituals releases a cocktail of serotonin and other "feel-good" chemicals in the brain.

Jordan Grafman, head of the cognitive neuroscience laboratory at Rehabilitation Institute of Chicago and neurology professor at Northwestern University, disagrees with the contention that humans have a "God spot." Instead, he maintains that belief in a higher power is embedded in a whole range of other belief systems in the brain that we use every day. Because religious beliefs and rituals are found in all cultures with no animal equivalent, he supports contemporary psychological theories that ground religious belief in evolutionary-adaptive cognitive functions and maintains that the human brain has evolved to be sensitive to any idea or cognitive process that improves our survival.

After analyzing subjects who had been asked to think about religious and moral problems and questions. Grafman found that people of different religious persuasions and beliefs, as well as atheists, all tended to use the same neural circuits to solve moral dilemmas. They observed activation in several areas of the brain, one within the frontal lobes of the cortex – which are unique to humans – and another in the more evolutionary-ancient regions deeper inside the brain, which humans share with apes and other primates. Highly religious people use this same circuitry when considering issues related to God or practicing religious rituals such as prayer or spiritual meditation. Grafman finds the relationship between religion and brain development to be reciprocal. "The human brain developed the capacity to establish social communities and behaviors, which are the basis of religious societies. But religious practice, in turn, developed the brain. As these societies became more cooperative, our brains evolved in response to that. Our brain led to behavior and then the behavior fed back to our brain to help sculpt it."

Regardless of where religion lives in the brain, whether it is the product of evolution or the byproduct of one's DNA, there is an undeniable connection between religion, meditation, and prayer and overall well-being. Numerous studies show that religious belief is physically, psychologically, and socially beneficial. Churchgoers live longer, have lower blood pressure, recover quicker from illness, have better outcomes from coronary disease and have greater success with in-vitro fertilization. People with a deep personal belief in God recover 70% faster from clinical depression than nonbelievers.

While the study of neurotheology is controversial, most researchers agree that neuroscience is a crucial area of research within the larger conversation around understanding religion. Neurotheologists contend that the objective of this field of study is not to discredit religion or diminish the positive impact of religion on individuals or society. Exploring the neurological processes of religiosity doesn't negate the existence or faith in a higher power. But maybe it does illuminate an evolutionary advantage, not in the belief of God, but in the brain circuitry involved in religious experiences and human's capacity to believe in God. One thing is certain: the more we learn about how spirituality and religiosity work in the brain and impact health, relationships and happiness, the more questions we uncover.

"A happy man is too satisfied with the present to dwell too much on the future."

The Science of Stress

Extremely traumatic events like the 9/11 attack on the World Trade Center or the Parkland school shooting are profoundly memorable. Even if not personally impacted, those aware of these kinds of events find them stressful to process. Even remembering where we were when we first heard the news can trigger a similar stress reaction. For most of us, however, the day-to-day stressors tend to do greater damage to our bodies and brains. Most stress is caused by the anticipation of a future event that will cause emotional or physical harm. Such stress doesn't feel good and can be frightening, making us irritable, grumpy, distracted and possibly even hostile.

Eliminating stress completely is impossible. A certain amount of stress actually keeps people alive and facilitates learning. Understanding the emotional manifestations is key to managing the right kind of stress. Two emotions specifically associated with stress are fear and anger. Anger is an energizing emotion, while fear is an energy-draining emotion, but both cause the release of cortisol. Whether that cortisol gives us an edge or becomes a handicap depends upon how much and for how long stress is present. For example, consider this scenario. On a business trip in New York City, walking back to the hotel from dinner one evening, Don experiences the eerie feeling of being followed. A glance back reveals a man following. Walking paces increase for both, and fear increases as the man following gets closer. Panic is setting in when this person calls out to stop and taps on Don's shoulder; Don then realizes it is the man from the restaurant. He hands over a credit card and says, "You left this on the table, and it's such a hassle to lose a credit card." Don exhales with relief and his brains sends the "all clear" signal enabling him to regain a sense of calm. What happens after the stressful event is over is the key to understanding whether it works for us or against us.

There are two primary types of stress, acute stress and chronic stress. Acute stress is the most common form stemming from the ordinary demands and pressures of life. A certain amount of acute stress keeps people alive and keeps the brain active and primed for high performance. Being aware of oncoming traffic, rushing to meet a deadline, worrying about losing a client, or missing work because of a sick child are all examples of acute stress. A healthy brain kicks into alert mode to deal with the event and eventually shifts back to a sense of calm when the danger or stress has been managed.

A wealth of research has been conducted to understand how this kind of stress can affect learning and memory. An intense stressor will result in the release of norepinephrine, which plays a role in the in the fight-or-flight response and triggers a host of physiological reactions. Studies show, however, that acute stress can also have profound effects on attention, working memory, and long-term memory, depending upon the specific memory stage affected and the proximity between the stressful event and the memory formation or retrieval. In addition, when faced with uncertainty and stress with a sense of resilience, we are motivated to find novel resolutions or adaptations.

Learning is highly dependent upon arousal level. Too little arousal results in less motivation to learn. Too much arousal creates neural "noise" that inhibits learning. People who are able to manage their stress levels also manage their arousal levels. Maximum learning occurs with a moderate level of arousal, and this level facilitates neuroplasticity through the production of new brain cells and neural connections.

UC Berkeley researchers Daniela Kaufer and Elizabeth Kirby maintain that controlled amounts of acute stress can lead to neurogenesis and prime the brain for improved performance. Recent studies on rats found that inter- mittent stressful events, short bursts with periods of calm in between, triggered the release of fibroblast growth proteins, which, in turn, led to the growth of new neurons. Two weeks later, those mature neurons improved the rats' mental performance. While the study of stress and new- cell growth is still being explored, scientists agree that regulated stress creates the optimum conditions for behavioral and cognitive performance. The key is how much stress, how long it lasts, and how well we manage it.

People who get stuck in acute stress and never give their brains a chance to shift back to calm mode suffer from what psychologists refer to as *episodic acute stress*. These are folks who seem to live in conditions of constant chaos and disorder. They are always in a hurry, late, nervous about something, putting out fires, or seeing disaster around every corner. If left untreated, episodic acute stress can lead to migraine headaches, hypertension, and even heart disease. More severe cases can lead to chronic stress with a long list of symptoms and illnesses.

Chronic stress is ongoing, overwhelming, and often debilitating, the feeling of powerlessness over what are perceived to be creating unrelenting demands and pressure. Chronic-stress reactions are similar to the symptoms of post-traumatic stress disorder, and they are exacerbated as people get used to them. Over time, as stress becomes the norm, it can significantly impact personality.

People with deep-seated convictions that the world is a dangerous place or they aren't good enough or smart enough or strong enough to overcome any kind of obstacle create a dark mental model and a destructive self-image – a dangerous state when it goes on so long that it becomes comfortable. After weeks, months, or even years of living in a chronic state of alarm, the stress reactions no longer protect us but instead have the unintended effect of intensifying traumatic memories and keeping them in the present.

Some cases of chronic stress stem from traumatic child-hood experiences, but poverty, abusive relationships or even being unhappy at work can all create the kind of ongoing stress that literally kills people. The vast majority of doctor visits, more than 90%, are for stress-related illnesses. Because both physical and mental resources are gradually depleted, chronic stress sufferers are much more likely to die of suicide, heart attack, stroke, and even cancer.

With any stress, fear, or anxiety, the brain is designed to put the entire body in motion to address it. At the first sign of danger, the brain activates the pituitary gland, the hypothalamus, and the adrenal glands. Within minutes, the hormones cortisol, adrenaline, and epinephrine are released into the blood stream.

With acute stress, one is able to recognize the danger, deal with it appropriately, and stop the flow of chemicals, thus regaining a sense of calm when the situation is over. Those who suffer from chronic stress are unable to return to a calm and peaceful state, so the brain continues to pump out cortisol, adrenaline, and epinephrine.

An overproduction of these hormones makes the body more vulnerable to everything from headaches, colds, and disease to impaired cognitive function. The greater the stress, the more cortisol is produced. The more cortisol that is produced, the more damage it does to the body over time.

10 Ways Stress Impacts the Brain and Body

1. The overproduction of cortisol can cause high blood pressure and heart attacks. Cortisol constricts the arteries, and epinephrine increases heart rate, which forces the heart to pump harder and faster.

2. Cortisol induces the production of glutamate, the neurotransmitter that creates free radicals that pierce the brain cell walls and cause them to rupture and die.

3. Too much cortisol decreases the production of BDNF (brain-derived neurotrophic factor). BDNF is the body's natural fertilizer designed to keep existing brain cells healthy and to stimulate neurogenesis.

4. Cortisol shrinks cells and inhibits neural generation in the hippocampus, which is responsible for episodic memory, learning, and the ability to regulate emotions.

5. Too much cortisol creates architectural changes in the prefrontal cortex, which impacts executive decision-making and impulsivity control.

6. Stress has been called "public enemy #1" because it leads to a host of other health issues including weight gain, heart disease, diabetes, digestive problems, sleeping disorders, skin afflictions, and cancer.

7. Stress builds up in the "fear center," or amygdala, and increases the neural connections in this part of the brain, which perpetuates a vicious cycle of stress and anxiety. That cycle creates more cortisol, and that cortisol creates more stress and anxiety.

8. Stress weakens the immune system, increasing one's vulnerability to anything from a common cold to more-severe autoimmune diseases.

9. Stress reduces the production of the "feel-good" chemicals, serotonin and dopamine, and in turn causes depression and is linked to addictive behaviors.

10. Stress shrinks the brain and kills brain cells.

Read that last line again.

Be you stressed or be you smart, no one can be both at the same time long term.

Have you ever noticed how people who are constantly stressed seem to be sick all the time? Cortisol partially shuts down the immune system when levels are high making the body susceptible to invasive pathogens. Bones and muscles are also affected. Cortisol inhibits amino acid levels in the muscle cells impeding their fuel source and decreases the calcium absorption in the intestines resulting in improper bone formation.

"We know from daily life that we exist for other people first of all, for whose smiles and well-being our own happiness depends."

Wired to Connect

Did you know that, compared to other species in the animal kingdom, the human brain is the largest relative to body size? Brain size typically correlates with body size across the animal kingdom. Elephants have huge bodies and huge brains while squirrels have small bodies and small brains. But humans are the exception to the rule.

With respect to the size of our bodies, our brains should be much smaller. Scientists have debated about why this is for a long time, but the research is fairly conclusive that the brain size of species correlates to the relevance of social connectedness. Humans have the largest brains relative to body size because we have the strongest need to connect with others.

Neuroscientists believe that attachment is such a primal need that there are networks of neurons in the brain dedicated to setting it in motion, and that process of forming lasting bonds is powered in part by oxytocin. Oxytocin, often called the "cuddle drug" is not just released during sex and skin-to-skin contact. The brain also releases it in non-intimate situations, like the platonic touches we experience in healthy friendships, social interactions, and even the feeling of belonging.

Numerous studies have examined the physical and psychological effects of human interaction or the lack thereof. A 2015 meta-analysis of 148 studies and found that greater social connection is associated with a 50% reduced risk of early death. Another meta-analysis of 70 studies found that social isolation and loneliness had the same effect on early death as obesity.

If we were to put a price tag on our relationships, it would be easier to recognize the value of our social connections. Social psychologists maintain that if you feel a deep meaningful connection with someone, it's like earning $100,000 more each year. Enjoying positive relationships at work feels like $60,000 more. On the other hand, when an important social tie is broken, like a divorce or the loss of an important friend, it feels like losing a job altogether.

One doesn't have to be a scientist to know the pain of social rejection. But to quantify it, neuroscientists set up an experiment to observe neural activity when people are rejected. Researchers asked participants to play a video game called Cyberball, tossing a ball around to each other as researchers monitored their brain activity.

At first, the facilitators tossed the ball to participants in turn. At a certain point, though, they excluded the participants from the game. Even though the participants knew that this was just a video game in a research study, they felt real distress by the exclusion. They genuinely felt rejected.

The most interesting part of the study is how their brains processed the social rejection. The stronger the feelings of rejection the subject reported, the greater neural activity in the part of the brain that processes physical pain.

Pain in the Brain

The brain itself does not feel pain because there are no pain receptors in brain tissue like those in the skin, joints, muscles, and some organs. This explains why neuro-surgeons can perform brain surgery without causing a patient discomfort, and, in some cases, even while the patient is awake. The brain is, however, what enables us to feel pain.

For example, imagine you're walking along the beach and you step on a broken shell. You don't actually feel the pain until receptors in your skin send a signal through the nerve into the spinal cord and eventually to your brain. All of this happens within a fraction of a second resulting in... OUCH! Immediately, the brain releases chemicals called opioids into the space between neurons in an effort to mute the pain signals. The more opioids that are released, the faster the pain dissipates.

Scientists have discovered that the brain doesn't distinguish between physical pain and social pain. We now know the same chemicals are released when we feel rejected, ridiculed, or isolated from others. Recent research conducted at the Molecular and Behavioral Neuroscience Institute at the University of Michigan discovered that the brain pathways that are activated during physical pain are the same as those activated during social pain. Using advanced brain scanning, they tracked the opioid release as the subjects experienced social rejection. The effect was the most pronounced in the same brain regions involved with physical pain.

Edward Smith, a psychologist at Columbia University in New York City, specifically examined how the brain processes rejection from a romantic relationship or meaningful friendship. MRI scans showed activation in the same brain areas that manage physical pain when subjects were asked to look at photographs of their ex-partners and recall the experience of being rejected. Even more striking, the team analyzed 150 other brain-scan experiments on negative social emotions such as fear, sadness, and anger. They found that none of these emotions activate the brain's physical sensory areas the way rejection from a relationship does.

Other studies show that reasoning and problem-solving abilities are significantly impacted when the brain is processing rejection. According to research conducted at Case Western Reserve University, participants who were actively dealing with personal experiences of rejection demonstrated an immediate drop in reasoning by 30% and in IQ by 25%. And, because we recall emotional rejection more strongly than physical pain, the brain tends to process social pain longer and more intensely than physical pain.

This shared brain circuitry for social and physical pain has important implications for learning and overall well-being. We are social creatures, and the brain processes any threat to our social connectedness the same way it processes a threat to our physical safety. We wouldn't tell a child who has a toothache to ignore it, nor would we tell a coworker who suffers from a herniated disc after falling in the stairway not to be so sensitive. And, we wouldn't tell a friend who breaks a leg to just think about the other leg.

Yet, often it's that same kind of advice given to the bullied child, the excluded coworker, and the rejected friend by well-intentioned people. Furthermore, people who experience multiple forms of social pain at the same time feel the same intensity of pain as those who suffer multiple physical injuries. The person who feels ridiculed by a coworker, rejected by a friend, and ignored by a spouse or partner simultaneously is in the same kind of pain as someone who has a toothache, a herniated disc, and a broken leg all at the same time. Perhaps a better understanding of how emotional pain is processed is the first step in learning how to show greater compassion and empathy.

Technology today makes it possible for us to be more connected, yet our social connections have actually decreased. Over the last 50 years, we've seen a downward trend in volunteering. People know fewer of neighbors. Fewer people are getting married. And we have fewer close friends with whom we'd share the intimate details of our lives. Over the same period of time, rates of suicide and clinical depression have never been higher.

According to the American Psychological Association, over 42.6 million Americans over the age of 45 live with chronic loneliness. People are feeling less social connectedness and more isolation than ever before. Perhaps the worst part of loneliness and social pain is the self-fulfilling cycle it creates. The more social pain one feels, the more one withdraws. The more one withdraws, the lonelier one feels.

The desire to be in a loving relationship, to fit in at school or within a church community, to avoid rejection and loss, to have someone in your life with whom you can share good news or bad news, all of these things have a significant impact on thoughts, actions, and feelings. And just knowing that you are important to another person is manifested in not just your happiness, but your overall physical and emotional well-being.

As an educator, it was important to me that my students were happy in my classroom and genuinely enjoyed learning. What I didn't realize then was how much stress and social pain significantly impacted their cognitive function and ability to learn. The same is true for adults. Beyond just making us sad, stress, rejection, loneliness and isolation all physically and chemically change the structure of the brain, impeding problem-solving, decision-making, creative thinking, productivity and memory. We are social creatures, and the ability to regulate stress and emotional pain in a healthy way gives us an edge in all of those tasks.

Understanding *how* we learn is the key to unlocking brain power and happiness. Having learned about learning, my challenge for you is to find ways to keep the good chemicals flowing: laugh a little more and stress a little less. Connect with people who make you feel good. Make time for a cup of coffee with a friend or send a text just to make someone smile. Nurture curiosity and learn how to ask different questions and to see things differently. Embrace mistakes as opportunities for growth, and get some sleep. Just imagine the Rockefeller Center tree growing up there! Check it out... you're a smarter YOU already!

FINDING THE JOY IN LEARNING

In a letter to his then 11-year-old son, Albert Einstein described the importance in finding the joy in learning. "That is the way to learn the most, that when you are doing something with such enjoyment that you don't notice that the time passes." As it turns out, Dr. Einstein was right again!

Brain maps of electrical activity (EEG or brain waves) and neuroimaging of neurotransmitters show us what happens when we experience learning with these positive emotions. We can actually see bursts of brain activity in one area of the brain followed by bursts of electrical activity in the hippocampus, amygdala, and other parts of the limbic system. When one finds joy in learning, the brain releases dopamine and acetylcholine. Think of this as a memory, focus, and attention-span cocktail.

"We cannot solve our problems
with the same kind of thinking
we used when we
created them."

Part II

Thinking about Thinking

Understanding the regions of the brain and how those structures process incoming data and communicate with the rest of the body is essential to learning how the brain works. That understanding, however, is only part of the equation.

Sigmund Freud's iceberg analogy describes our three levels of the mind. The conscious mind, all of the mental processes of which we are aware, is the tip of the iceberg. The level just below consciousness is the preconscious, or our available memory. As an example, it's unlikely that you are thinking about your address as you read this page, but just mentioning it brings it into your consciousness.

Like an iceberg, the most important part of the mind is the part you cannot see. Fueled by powerful neuroimaging technology, scientists now have the ability to explore the unconscious mind to discover neural codes and processes that explain how we make snap decisions, where gut feelings live, what inspires us, and what motivates us.

According to cognitive neuroscientists, the unconscious mind is the primary source of human behavior, managing 95% of cognitive activity. What separates us from other living creatures is our ability to create personal narratives from the frameworks of experiences stitched together with our underlying assumptions from values, beliefs, education, and relationships. These narratives don't just shape our view of the world; they become deeply ingrained mental models of how we define personal growth, vulnerability, gratitude, happiness and success.

Beyond intelligence and cognitive function, why do some people have the ability to power through uncertainty, chaos, and failure to achieve greatness and find greater happiness while others cry "uncle"? Why are we more honest after seeing the Disney logo? What makes us feel compelled to help a stranger? Why are optimists more successful salespeople? Why do we procrastinate? Welcome to your unconscious mind. From blinking to pushing the grocery cart without crashing into the candy shelves to having an "aha" moment in the shower, most of what we do every minute of every day is powered by the unconscious.

It's time to start thinking about thinking.

"The most beautiful thing we can experience is the mysterious. It is the source of all true art and science."

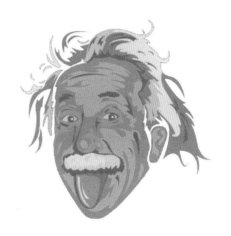

Hidden Powers in the Unconscious Mind

In every cognitive process, there are instantaneous and subconscious processes also at work. The exact nature of the subconscious mind on cognitive function has been a topic of debate; however, that the subconscious plays a role in cognition is undeniable among neuroscientists, psychologists, and linguists. Some argue that the unconscious mind is often more efficient and efficacious than the conscious mind, especially when there are multiple data points to consider.

Numerous studies show that the unconscious mind gathers and processes information much faster than the conscious brain; however, we can influence what happens in the subconscious without even realizing it. An excellent example of this is called *priming.*

Priming refers to the exposure of one stimulus that influences the reaction to a subsequent one. Without conscious awareness, the brain makes representations or associations that often shape our thoughts or actions. The concept of priming is not new. Vance Packard pioneered the research of it in his then groundbreaking book, *The Hidden Persuaders,* published in 1959.

Specifically, he explored the psychological and subliminal manipulation used in advertising. Since then, a wealth of research has illuminated how priming not only creates an association that influences thoughts and emotions, but it also affects our behavior through environmental cues that we see or hear as well as simple intentional actions. All of the sensory stimuli we process influence us in a variety of ways, and many times we are completely unaware.

For example, Apple has cultivated a brand personality synonymous with nonconformity and creativity. Apple connected on an emotional level with the famous "Think Different" campaign featuring images of Einstein, John Lennon, Gandhi, and Dr. Martin Luther King. They celebrated "the crazy ones...pushing the human race forward," and spotlighted "the people who are crazy enough to think they can change the world."

But, their brand personality influences more than consumer spending and a cult-like following. A 2008 study conducted by Grainne Fitzsimons and Tanya Chartrand found that priming people with an Apple logo made them think more creatively in a simple task on "unusual uses for a brick," while people primed with an IBM logo produced less-creative results. Not only did participants associate Apple with creativity, they actually demonstrated greater creativity when primed with the logo.

The same study sought to determine if brands could influence character traits such as honesty and sincerity. They determined that the Disney Channel brand was highly associated with honesty in a preliminary survey. The E! Channel brand served as the control. Participants didn't associate E! Channel with honesty but liked it to a similar degree as Disney Channel. To measure honesty, they administered a social desirability test designed to present conflicts between the desire to respond honestly and the desire to respond in a way that made them appear more socially desirable.

They found that the people primed with the Disney logo demonstrated greater honesty than those primed with the E! logo. Disney prompted them to admit to engaging in more undesirable behaviors and claimed to engage in fewer unrealistic socially desirable behaviors.

Communication scientists San Bolkan and Peter Andersen explored this concept in a survey experiment to determine whether people could be primed to participate in a voluntary task. They asked people walking through a mall to stop and answer a few survey questions. In the first test, only 29% participated. In the second test, they approached people with a question: "Do you consider yourself a helpful person?" Almost every participant answered yes. Then the researchers asked them to take the survey. Participation jumped to 77%. That simple question primed people to demonstrate just how helpful they were.

Researchers at New York University wanted to find out if cognitive priming would shape behavior by just seeing certain words. They divided subjects into two groups and asked them to complete a series of word puzzles. One group was given puzzles that included words associated with kindness and patience while the other group received word searches filled with words related to impolite behavior.

After they finished the puzzles, the researchers asked the subjects to speak with a lab assistant who was pretending to be on the phone. Those who completed the puzzles that included the words related to impolite behavior waited less time to interrupt the lab assistant than those who were exposed to words related to kindness and patience. This example of priming shows how merely seeing certain words influences thought and behavior.

Hearing words can have the same effect. In another study, researchers used words associated with the elderly like *old*, *wrinkled*, and *tired* in conversation with one group of adults. They used age-neutral words in conversation with another group. The group primed with the elderly words walked away more slowly and reported having lower energy after the conversation than those primed with the age-neutral words. Just hearing words related to the aged primed that group to feel and act older!

A host of physical and emotional effects are triggered when we view images that convey belonging, nurturing, and human connection. Research proves that images depicting physical touch, kindness, or a sense of safety increase resilience to stress and prime the brain for positive prosocial behaviors like care, compassion, and helpfulness. Researchers Harriet Over and Malinda Carpenter of Germany's Max Planck Institute explored the priming effect of affiliation. Specifically, they wanted to see if affiliation cues would influence group identity and belonging demonstrated by an increase in helpful behavior. Subjects were shown a series of photos showing familiar household objects with one of four primes in the background: two wooden dolls together, one wooden doll alone, two wooden dolls back to back or two stacks of wooden blocks serving as a control.

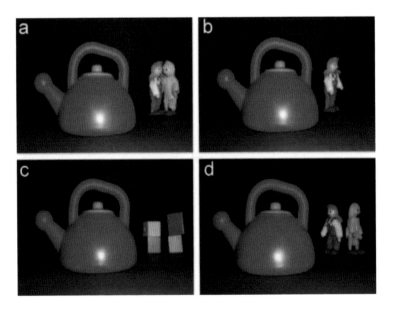

The researcher named the object, color, and function in each photograph but completely ignored the prime in the background. After the presentation of the pictures, the researcher left the room momentarily and returned with a bundle of six small sticks and "accidentally" dropped them on the floor. During the first ten seconds after dropping the sticks, the experimenter said nothing. Some of the subjects began to help her pick up the sticks. During the next ten seconds, the experimenter looked at the subjects who hadn't started helping and said, "I dropped my sticks on the floor."

The results showed that in the first ten seconds after dropping the sticks, those primed with the together figures spontaneously helped three times more than each of the other three conditions. The together prime prompted helpful behavior. But, even more remarkable is the fact that the subjects were 18-month-old infants!

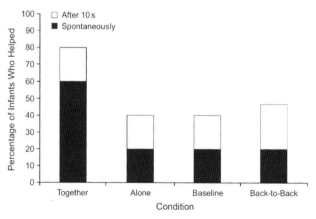

Fig. 2. Percentage of infants who helped the experimenter spontaneously (i.e., during the first 10 s) and during the rest of the test phase (i.e., including after prompting) in each of the four conditions.

Even simple actions can influence our emotions and moods. For example, college students were asked to read a series of *The Far Side* cartoons and rate them on humor. One group was asked to read them while holding a pencil horizontally between their teeth, forcing a smiling expression. A second group was asked to read them holding a pencil vertically, forcing a frowning expression. Those holding a pencil between their teeth horizontally rated the same cartoons significantly funnier than the other group.

Psychologist, Daniel Kahneman replicated this experiment during his speech at the 2013 World Economic Forum in Davos. Those who held the pencil horizontally, forcing a smiling expression, reported higher levels of happiness and light-heartedness than those who held the pencil vertically, forcing a frowning expression. Kahneman maintains that cause and effect often operate in a reciprocal manner.

"Being amused tends to make you smile and smiling tends to make you feel amused."

-Daniel Kahneman

This experiment demonstrates that the brain is wired for priming; it isn't something that we learn. It also opens up a wealth of possibilities for future research including how subtle changes to the environment can positively prime anyone and promote prosocial behavior. It can be a tool or a weapon, and we need to tread lightly on the thin line between positive priming and potential manipulation of ourselves and others. The good news is that there are some very simple ways to utilize cognitive priming with the intention to get the outcome you seek.

But first, let's dig into what is actually happening in the brain during priming. Thinking isn't a linear process; thinking is a *linking* process. Data doesn't simply come in through the senses and travel to various regions of the brain like stops on a bus route before finally producing a thought, emotion, or behavior. Instead, groups of neurons are continually processing numerous pieces of data simultaneously. To do this efficiently, the brain looks for patterns and associations. Those patterns and associations are the building blocks for thought.

For example, when you have a conversation with someone, your brain doesn't just wait to hear what is spoken. The unconscious mind is busy predicting what is likely to be expressed next. It looks for patterns and processes syntax, meaning, intonation, body language and all of the other dynamics of a conversation. At the same time, it is also predicting patterns in other neural branches that are simultaneously being activated by sensory stimuli.
Even when you read a group of words, your brain looks for a pattern. For example, read the following list of words:

- romantic
- passion
- beautiful
- desire

Now, complete these words by filling in the missing letters:

- L _ _ E
- K _ _ S

It's more likely than not that you added letters to form the words *love* and *kiss*. You could have filled in the letters to create a number of other words – lane, line, lake, keys, kits, kegs – but none of them fit the pattern primed by the first set of words. When the senses perceive any form of stimuli, the brain automatically looks for patterns and associations that form thoughts and influence behaviors.

So, how can we use priming to our advantage? There are many ways to consciously influence the unconscious mind. For example, if you start your day reading news about crime, explosions, protests, child abuse, or other awful things in the world, you have unwittingly primed your brain for danger, fear, and stress. On the other hand, if you start your day with the practice of gratitude, identifying those people, places, and things for which you are grateful, you prime your brain with love, affection, belonging, and other positive emotions.

Priming is a great way to make your work environment a bastion of productivity, creativity, or positivity. Create the links and associations that will prime your brain with inspiring images or words that connote the outcome you want. Little things like a sticky note with the word *success* or *focus* strategically placed so that it is in view without being a distraction is a very simple first step. Quotes are another great way to prime the brain with empowering mental mantras.

Another simple strategy is to build a digital portfolio of the future you want. This could be as simple as a folder that is easily accessible on your computer desktop. Add pictures or videos that represent what is important to you, the life you want, and what makes you feel alive. What do you want to spend more time doing? With whom do you want to spend more time? What new things do you want to learn? Every now and again, scroll though those pictures and prime your brain with the life you want to live.

The Illusory-Truth Effect

The illusory-truth effect is another example of the subconscious mind at work. Also known as the reiteration effect, this phenomenon explains a glitch in the human psyche that equates repetition with credibility. The illusory-truth effect was first observed by a research team led by Lynn Hasher at the University of Toronto in 1977. They discovered that people rated repeated statements as "more probably true" than new statements. Hasher's team asserted that assessment of truth is dependent upon two things: how well the statement aligns with what we already believe to be true and how familiar it is.

To illustrate the illusory effect, consider a 2012 study conducted by Danielle Polage at Central Washington University regarding fake news and political propaganda. Subjects were exposed to false news stories presented as true. Five weeks later, those who had read the fake news stories rated them as more truthful than those who had not.

The results also revealed that even though participants were aware that they had been exposed to the story during the experiment, they believed that they had heard or read about the story somewhere else. Repeating false claims not only increases believability, but it often results in the false belief that these stories had been heard previously and from more than one source or a highly credible source.

A 2018 study conducted at MIT, the largest fake news study to date, corroborated how rapidly misinformation spreads via social media. Researchers found that the truth takes six times longer to be seen than misinformation and lies were 70% more likely to be shared than the truth, even when controlled for factors like verified accounts, the number of followers, and how long the account had been active.

Furthermore, while bots are often blamed for the spread of fake news online, the researchers found a negligible impact. Researchers concluded, "[False] news spreads farther, faster, deeper, and more broadly than the truth because humans, not robots, are more likely to spread it."

Although an illogical basis for truth, repetition increases familiarity, and familiarity can be more powerful than rational thought processes. It's called *cognitive fluency*, and when we see or hear a statement or story a second time or a third time, it's much easier to process. The unconscious brain interprets the ease and speed with which it is processed as evidence that the information is true.

Furthermore, repeatedly hearing a known falsehood can have a paradoxical effect. It eventually becomes so familiar that it reaches a tipping point where it is accepted as truth even when it was initially accepted as false.

"The truth of any proposition has nothing to do with its credibility and vice versa."

-Parker's Law of Political Statements

The ease with which the brain processes information doesn't just determine credibility. It also determines appeal. When we process something with cognitive ease, we perceive it more positively and the smiling muscles engage. Researchers Winkielman and Cacioppo conducted an experiment using EMG (electromyography) technology. They found a significant correlation between cognitive fluency and the smiling muscle activity. Conversely, those participants who processed more-difficult information engaged the frowning muscle activity.

Other studies have substantiated the correlation between fluency and appeal. Research shows that easy-to-process information, anything from a collection of stamps to items on a Chinese menu, is evaluated more positively than information that is difficult to process. Stocks that are easy to pronounce generally perform better, and drugs with easy-to-read names are perceived to be safer and more effective.

Studies even show that statements that rhyme are more persuasive, judged more accurately and more memorable than statements that do not rhyme. It's called the *rhyme-as-reason effect,* or Eaton-Rosen phenomenon, and it's a known persuasion technique commonly used in marketing and advertising. No doubt you're familiar with some of them:

Alka Selzer: Plop, plop, fizz, fizz, oh what a relief it is!
Timex: It takes a lickin' and keeps on tickin'
Electrolux: Nothing sucks like an Electrolux.

Researcher, Petra Filkukova investigated the rhyme-as-reason effect on fictitious advertising slogans. Subjects were asked to judge between rhyming and non-rhyming sayings. They not only found the rhyming sayings more likeable but also more trustworthy and better suited to the products and campaigns they were meant to advertise.

Another study conducted by Matthew McGlone and his team, subjects were presented with a series of statements. In each case, half the study participants received statements that rhymed, for example, "caution and measure will win you treasure" and "sobriety conceals what alcohol reveals" and the other half got non-rhyming versions of the same statements: "caution and measure will win you riches" and "sobriety conceals what alcohol unmasks".

Participants were asked to rate how accurately each reflected the real world. Even though participants maintained the belief that rhyming was in no way an indication of accuracy, they still rated those that rhymed as more accurate than those that didn't.

Some experts have even theorized that the rhyme-as-reason effect may have been at work in the O.J. Simpson trial with one critical statement made by Johnny Cochran in his closing argument: "If it doesn't fit, you must acquit." (That wasn't the only time Cochran employed the persuasive power of rhyme. In an effort to repair his reputation as a publicity-hungry lawyer after the trial, he said, "I work not only for the OJs, but also for the No Js.")

The principle of cognitive fluency even shows up in the way we perceive people based upon the ease with which we can pronounce their names. People who have names that are easy to pronounce are judged more positively than people with names that are difficult to pronounce. In a 2011 study, Simon Laham and his colleagues sought to determine whether this phenomenon extended to professional success.

Specifically, they examined the names of 500 American lawyers collected from the websites of ten U.S. firms varying in size from the largest firm to the 178th largest firm. Their analysis showed that lawyers with easily pronounced names occupied higher positions within their firm than those with names that were difficult to pronounce. This effect was consistent regardless of firm size, firm ranking, or mean-associate salary.

The principles of cognitive fluency also apply to the way information is presented in print. In one study, researchers asked participants to read instructions on how to do an exercise routine. The instructions were printed in two different fonts—a font that was easy to read and a font that was more difficult to read.

When participants were asked to estimate how long it would take to actually perform the exercise routine, they estimated it would take about 8 minutes to perform the exercise after reading the instructions in the font that was easy to read compared to 15 minutes in the font more difficult to read. They also found the exercise program that was easier to read to be more appealing and, therefore, more willing to incorporate it into their daily activities.

In another study, researchers presented information about two different phones in a font that was easy to read or a font that was more difficult to read. While only 17% of the participants postponed making a decision when the product information was in the font that was easy to read, 41% postponed making a decision when the information was in a font that was difficult to read. Subconsciously, people attributed the complexity of the font with the complexity of the decision itself.

"Give people more experience at pronouncing and working with names from different backgrounds, and in its small way, it could contribute to reducing prejudice."

- Dr. Simon Laham

"Only those who attempt the absurd can achieve the impossible."

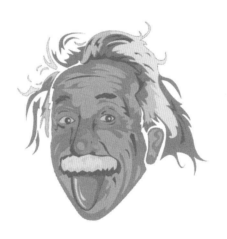

Fears, Commas, and the F-Word

Recently, I heard someone say that life should be about commas, not periods. It was one of those sticky thoughts that bounced around my head. To put it in context, this person was talking about personal struggles such as losing a job, a troubled relationship, health issues, whatever mountain loomed ahead. The question he asked that kept nudging me was, "Does that mountain seem so big that you put a period and call it a day, or do you put a comma and keep climbing?" Sometimes those mountains seem huge, and sometimes it takes courage to put a comma and keep climbing because of that scary four-letter F-word: FAIL. What if I can't do it? What if I FAIL?

Professionally or personally, no one likes to fail. Some fear failure so much that it becomes debilitating, and there is a name for that: atychiphobia, a fear of failure, number 15 on the list of the top 100 phobias. A person who has atychiphobia has an irrational and persistent fear of failure so intense that the risk is not worth the potential reward, putting a period on possibilities, opportunities, and growth. We're taught at a very young age that the brightest kids get the right answers. Wrong answers are evidence that we aren't smart. As adults, intellectually we know that mistakes are essential to the learning process, but no one wants to make them, let alone embrace them or shine a light on them. Research conducted over the last decade or so has investigated the interplay between talent and effort and success and failure.

Surveys show that most people claim effort outranks talent and perseverance is more valuable than intelligence. Intellectually, people will admit that, at some point, we all encounter something we don't know or can't do. But, let's be honest. Most of us want the world to see us as the talented and accomplished genius rather than the guy who works hard, fails a lot, but eventually gets it right.

Theory researchers maintain that our aspirations and accomplishments have less to do with intelligence and talent and more to do with the way we feel about the F-word. How do you view failure? Do you fear it, or do you view it as a temporary setback? Do you avoid challenges, or do you seek them out? Do you feel smart when you're able to solve a problem quickly and easily or when you're able to figure it out after struggling with it? The people who start out the smartest are not always the most successful. Developing a growth mindset may be the key to embracing challenges as well as learning from the mistakes and failures that often accompany them. That means knowing when to use periods and when to use commas.

"Failure is success in progress."
-Albert Einstein

People with a fixed mindset use periods:

It is what it is.
There is nothing I can do about it.
Overcoming this is impossible.
I can't do it.

People with a growth mindset use commas:

That didn't work, so there must be another way.
I'm not done, and I'll be back tomorrow.
I don't know, but someone out there does.
I can't do it, yet.

Success Through Failure

Some of the world's greatest entrepreneurs, inventors, innovators, and visionaries claim they wouldn't have discovered success without their mistakes. Consider the journey of James Dyson, industrial design engineer and founder of the Dyson Company. Dyson maintains he discovered his biggest successes through failure. Before his first marketable Dual Cyclone vacuum cleaner in 1993, he made over 5,127 prototypes, or according to Dyson, "5,126 failures." He maintained that he could have never even imagined his final product without those failures.

In a 2007 interview with *Fast Company*, he said, "I've always thought that schoolchildren should be marked by the number of failures they've had. The child who tries strange things and experiences lots of failures to get there is going to be more creative."

Today, the company generates almost $5 billion in sales and employs 3,500 engineers around the world. Dyson acknowledges that not all failures turn into successes and clarifies that the key is to fail constructively. "If you want to discover something that other people haven't, you need to do things the wrong way. Initiate a failure by doing something that's very silly, unthinkable, naughty, dangerous. Paying attention to why it fails can take one on a completely different path."

Thomas Edison was also famous for succeeding at failing. His teachers told him he was "too stupid to learn anything." He was fired from his first two jobs before being hired by Western Union to work the Associated Press bureau newswire. At 19, he asked to be assigned to the night shift thinking it would give him the privacy to work on his inventions. When he accidentally spilled acid that dripped onto his boss's desk, he was fired. Two years later, he received his first patent for the electric vote recorder. He went on to hold more than 1,000 patents.

Walt Disney was fired from the *Kansas City Star* because his editor felt he "lacked imagination and had no good ideas." As an evening news anchor, Oprah Winfrey often became emotionally invested in her stories. Her producer not only fired her but publicly humiliated her saying she was "unfit for television." Lee Iacocca climbed to the top of the Ford Motor Company, but after a clash with Henry Ford Jr. and a series of failed ideas, he was fired. He took his passion and his ideas to Chrysler. Jerry Seinfeld, Steve Jobs, Steven Spielberg, Lee Iacocca... the list goes on.

What is it about those who use failures as stepping stones to success? Why are some people unafraid to fail or willing to take risks to reach their goals while others would rather play it safe? There is a wealth of research that suggests that success is not dependent upon a single factor like intelligence or work ethic but rather the combination of mindset, grit, passion, and the ability to be vulnerable.

Growth Mindset vs. Fixed Mindset

The human mind is a powerful narrator. The way we see ourselves and the stories we tell ourselves can either fuel success or sabotage it. That internal dialogue doesn't just impact our success; it influences the goals we set and the extent to which we will stretch to achieve them. Developing a growth mindset is the foundation for the sense of agency it takes to realize one's potential.

According to Stanford researcher Carol Dweck, the difference between what she calls a "fixed mindset" and a "growth mindset" determines what is learned and how well it is learned. Dweck maintains that a fixed mindset assumes our character, intelligence, and creativity are fixed traits over which we have no control. Those with a fixed mindset thrive only when everything is easy. A growth mindset is the belief that even though we each have unique talents, aptitudes, and interests, our mental traits can change through effort and experience. People with a growth mindset don't just accept challenges; they search for them. The bigger the challenge the better!

Dweck contrasts the two mindsets this way:

In a fixed mindset, students believe their basic abilities, their intelligence, their talents, are just fixed traits. They have a certain amount, and that's that, and then their goal becomes to look smart all the time and never look dumb. In a growth mindset, students understand that their talents and abilities can be developed through effort, excellent teaching, and persistence. They don't necessarily think everyone's the same or anyone can be Einstein, but they believe everyone can get smarter if they work at it.

-Carol Dweck, Stanford University

Mindset Influences How and What We Learn

Much of Dweck's research explores how these mindsets are formed in early childhood development. In a study on hundreds of school-age children, she examined how different types of praise are likely to influence mindset as well as how each mindset impacts learning and academic achievement. Some students were praised for how hard they worked on various tasks while others were praised for their ability.

Two critical findings stood out: (1) Praise that focuses on effort nurtures a growth mindset, while praise that focuses on ability nurtures a fixed mindset; and (2) Students with a fixed mindset will reject learning experiences to avoid failure. When students were asked to choose the tasks they wanted to complete, those who were praised for ability chose the most straightforward tasks. They declined to try more challenging tasks that could result in failure or spotlight their weaknesses. To these students, failure meant they were not smart and the risk of failing far outweighed the benefits of learning something new.

Conversely, those who were praised for effort weren't intimidated by the risk of failing difficult tasks. They embraced challenges. In fact, 90% of them wanted to tackle the most challenging tasks. To this group, failure was not a reflection of intellect or ability; instead, it was a source of motivation and an opportunity to get smarter.

The team expanded the research to find out if a fixed or growth mindset influences character traits such as honesty. They asked the students to write about their experience and disclose their scores on the tasks. Forty percent of the students in the ability-praised group inflated their scores to make them look more intelligent. Because a fixed mindset equates failure with intelligence, almost half of these students lied about their scores so that others wouldn't perceive them as stupid.

Dweck didn't confine her research to school-age children. She examined brainwaves of adults to determine how mindset affects the way people receive feedback. Those with a fixed mindset were much more interested in feedback about their ability. Those with a growth mindset, however, were more interested in learning how to improve their current ability. They defined ability as *where they are today* instead of *who they are*. The collective body of this research confirms that mindset is an influential factor in the willingness to learn as well as the ability to learn new things.

Organizational Mindset

Mindset research has been expanded over the last twenty years to explore whether an organization can cultivate a fixed or a growth mindset, and, if so, how such thinking impacts employee engagement and company culture. Any type of workplace environment, academic, business, nonprofits, and others, communicates a cultural mindset through shared norms and values. In correlation with a growth or fixed mindset, cultures can be defined as those of *genius* or *development*.

A culture of genius is the view that brilliance is the critical ingredient for success. These companies focus on finding the "rock stars," and their people learn quickly that they have to do whatever it takes to be smarter than the next guy. For example, consider this description of Enron:

It was a company that prized "sheer brainpower" above all else, where the task of sorting out "intellectual stars" from the "merely super-bright" was the top priority when making hires and promotions. It was an environment where one of the most powerful executives was described as being "so sure that he was the smartest guy in the room that anyone who disagreed with him was summarily dismissed as just not bright enough to 'get it.' "

–Description of Enron (McLean & Elkind, 2003)

This organization deemed that people were either intelligent or not, and little or no value was placed on growth, learning, or effort. Malcolm Gladwell called this mindset the "blueprint for Enron's culture and demise." In a piece published in *The New Yorker* a year after the Enron scandal, Gladwell wrote:

"The broader failing of McKinsey and its acolytes at Enron is their assumption that an organization's intelligence is simply a function of the intelligence of its employees. They believe in stars because they don't believe in systems. In a way, that's understandable, because our lives are so obviously enriched by individual brilliance. Groups don't write great novels, and a committee didn't come up with the theory of relativity. But companies work by different rules. They don't just create; they execute and compete and coordinate the efforts of many different people, and the organizations that are most successful at that task are the ones where the system is the star."

Gladwell maintains that companies with a genius mindset teach employees to define themselves and the company by that description. Genius creates value. When that image is threatened, employees would rather lie than admit to mistakes that might invalidate their value. Any opportunity for learning and self-correcting the system is sabotaged by the system. As Gladwell concludes, "They were there looking for people who had the talent to think outside of the box. It never occurred to them that, if everyone had to think outside the box, maybe it was the box that needed fixing."

Conversely, cultures of development embody the ability to learn and grow with a focus on resilience. These companies place a value on employees' abilities to set high goals and take risks to reach them. Consider this very different description of another company that was the target of SEC investigations, Xerox:

In public statements, executives proudly described their CEO's growth and learning over 35 years –from sales rep to the head of the organization. Managers expected their workers to show a passion and love for learning and expanding knowledge. Instead of proving how smart a person or division was, the company's focus was on facilitating contributions, investing in employees' experiences, developing a larger portion of talent, and intense on-the-job learning.

Description of Xerox (George & McLean, 2005; Vollmer, 2004; Knowledge@Wharton, 2005)

When Anne Mulcahy took over Xerox in 2000, it was $17 billion in debt with a stock value that had plummeted from $63.69 to $4.43 per share. On the very day her appointment was announced, the stock had dropped 15%. By 2003, however, it had delivered four straight profitable quarters.

Mulcahy hadn't been groomed to become a CEO, and she didn't have a sophisticated financial background. So how did she turn a company on the verge of collapse into what *Money* magazine called the "great turnaround story of the post-crash era"?

Mulcahy attributes the success to a company-wide focus on "intense on-the-job learning" starting at the top. She identified communication as the most important element of the turnaround strategy, and she expected full participation from every employee. "When I became CEO, I spent the first 90 days on planes traveling to various offices and listening to anyone who had a perspective on what was wrong with the company. I think if you spend as much time listening as talking, that's time well spent."

It's easy to see the difference between the genius and the development approach. Xerox created a team focused on its commitment to identifying problems and learning how to fix them together while Enron created a team focused on competing with one another, each striving to be the smartest guy in the room.

What is it like to function in an environment that values genius and talent over work ethic and achievement over contribution? How does the leader's mindset affect employee engagement and the culture of an organization? An emergence of research examines these questions as well as how these cultural mindsets inform employees' level of trust and commitment in the organization.

"Don't show up to prove. Show up to improve."
-Simon Sinek

Belonging is a fundamental human need. We all want to be accepted as a member of a family, group, team, classroom, community, organization, and more. To gain that acceptance, people subconsciously display the qualities believed to be valued by the other members of the group. For example, a member of an activist organization is much more likely to be vocal about political issues in that group than within his church community. Likewise, the persona displayed with golf buddies is likely to be different from one displayed at work.

When people apply for a job, they strive to espouse the attributes and characteristics that they believe are most valued in that organization. When a leader assumes an air of superiority, the good little soldiers dutifully fill the inferior roles. Furthermore, when people believe that a company prioritizes certain traits such as genius over development, there is a natural tendency to shift their self-concepts to reflect the values of the organization.

Research shows that even when people do not particularly like the organizational mindset, this mindset significantly influences the way they portray themselves, the way they see themselves, and the way they interact with others. It even carries over to how they evaluate others. William James, one of the leading thinkers of the 19th century, often called the "Father of American psychology," once said, "A person has as many different social selves as there are distinct groups of persons about whose opinion he cares."

A two-year study of Fortune 1000 companies was conducted by the culture-shaping firm, Senn Delaney, in collaboration with Dweck and her colleagues. To define the existing culture of the companies, employees were asked whether they thought their company had a culture of genius or culture of development. They also asked them to rate their agreement on statements about the company such as, "This company believes that people have a certain amount of talent, and they really can't do much to change it." High levels of agreement indicated the company had a fixed mindset; low levels suggested a growth mindset.

The researchers then surveyed the employees to see if there was a correlation between mindset and job satisfaction, employee engagement, collaboration, and perception of culture as well as whether it impacted managers' perceptions of employees. Employees in the culture of genius companies characterized the climate there as inequitable, mistrusting, and dishonest. They reported extreme competition and unethical behaviors such as "cheating, shortcuts, and cutting corners" as well as "hiding information and keeping secrets." Many felt that only a few employees were valued and respected and that the company largely didn't care about the rest. They worried about being called out for failing, so they stayed in their comfort zones and avoided taking risks that could result in creativity and innovation.

When people focus on trying to prove how smart they are, they often ignore, avoid, or abandon potentially valuable learning opportunities. Employees who feel that innovation and hard work are only rewarded if they are successful are much more likely to play it safe and fly under the radar.

Fixed-mindset companies are also prone to rely on stereotyping and thus attract a less-diverse applicant pool. In one study, researchers showed participants several hypothetical company websites to measure the level of appeal. The sites that portrayed fixed mindsets looking for employees "who have the intelligence and abilities we're looking for" were less appealing than those that focused on helping employees "learn, discover, and grow." Participants specifically cited a lack of trust in the fixed mindset companies.

Those employees describing their companies as having cultures of growth and development reported greater trust, a stronger commitment to the company, and stronger support for risk-taking, innovation, and creativity. They were 47% more likely to agree with statements related to trust in the company and 34% more likely to feel a sense of ownership and commitment to the success of the company. They also showed 65% stronger agreement that the company supported risk-taking and creative endeavors and 49% stronger agreement that they fostered innovative efforts.

Perhaps the most significant difference is in what people reported about initiative and change. In the genius cultures, people demonstrated a lack of initiative and an entrenched resistance to change. Those in cultures of development assumed ownership over making improvements and sought out how their role impacted the bigger picture. They were personally invested in contributing to the organizational goals.

Another study conducted by Laura Kray and Michael Haselhuhn examined how one's mindset impacted the ability to learn a vital business skill: negotiation. They divided MBA students who were in a negotiations course into two groups and delivered instruction with either a fixed mindset or a growth mindset. For example, the fixed group read articles like "Negotiation Ability, Like Plaster, Is Pretty Stable Over Time." The growth group read things like "Negotiation Ability is Changeable and Can Be Developed."

The students were asked to choose the negotiation tasks they wanted to complete. Some of the tasks were designed to showcase their skills but wouldn't teach them anything new. Other tasks were more challenging but designed to improve upon the skills they already had. Almost half of the fixed group chose the "show off" tasks compared to only 12% of the growth group. Overwhelmingly, the participants in the growth mindset group were more interested in learning how to improve their skills than showing off what they already knew.

Kray and Haselhuhn also discovered an interesting finding regarding how mindsets influence trust. Participants in the fixed group locked into their initial view of their negotiation partners. If a participant perceived the other to be trustworthy, the negotiator fixated on that view and believed it to be fact. Even when they knew they had been deceived, people with fixed mindsets tended to explain away or excuse deceptions. Likewise, if participants perceived their negotiation partners as untrustworthy, they held firm in that view despite evidence to the contrary.

Participants in the growth group formed an initial opinion about their negotiating partners but changed that opinion after realizing that opinion was inaccurate. Unlike the fixed group, they were able to incorporate information that conflicted with their original mental models to revise an opinion that could influence the deal. Overall, their findings demonstrated that the more a negotiator's mindset was one of growth, they were able to generate more creative solutions and more lucrative deals.

Cultivating a culture of development is key to developing an engaged, collaborative, innovative, and trusting workforce. It starts with leadership. Leaders who prioritize genius create an "every-man-for-himself" mentality. Employees will learn to make choices that center on how the boss will respond rather than how the company will benefit. Instead of using the organization as an engine for learning and growth, people become conditioned not to ask the hard questions, not to take risks for fear of failure, and not to share mistakes so that others might learn from them.

Growth leaders create opportunities for teaching and learning at all levels of the organization. These self-effacing people nurture contributions rather than competitions, and such leaders find success because they can confront failures and mistakes and then correct them rather than hide from missteps and possibly be defeated by them. When employees are encouraged to step out of their comfort zones without fear of being penalized for making mistakes along the way, engagement, collaboration, and innovation are natural rewards.

Whether human qualities such as the ability to learn or increase intellectual capacity are things that can be nurtured and developed or things that we're born with isn't a new concept. Most experts today will agree that it's not nature or nurture but rather the influence of both that determines how individual traits are developed. Of course, we all have a unique genetic blueprint, but research is proving that we have more capacity for learning and brain development than we ever thought possible. As Alfred Binet, the inventor of the IQ test, once said, "It's not always the people who start out the smartest who end up the smartest."

"The important thing is to not stop questioning. Curiosity has its own reason for existing."

Going to Bed Smarter than You Woke Up

Mindset and one's perceptions of failure and success are only part of the learning equation. The secret to building intellectual capacity has just as much to do with how we see ourselves in relation to those around us. Each of us lives in a filter bubble, an ideological cocoon that insulates us from opposing viewpoints while also distorting the way we see ourselves. It's a tug of war between two opposing and subconscious cognitive functions: *illusory superiority* and *affinity bias*.

Illusory superiority is a psychological quirk allowing us to believe we are better than most others, better drivers, more honest, more intelligent. Affinity bias refers to the natural tendency to like and surrounds ourselves with people who share similar beliefs or interests. Combined, these two cognitive functions often distort our sense of self and result in an inflated assessment of our "rightness" and the subconscious dismissal of any challenging opinions.

"Of course, I'm right! Everyone tells me so."

According to Warren Buffet and his longtime partner, Charlie Munger, the secret to going to bed smarter than you wake up is doing the work required to have an opinion *before* forming an opinion. Such a challenging task involves being surrounded by people who are not afraid to challenge ideas and having the intellectual humility to abandon a position if proven wrong. This challenging work counteracts our subconscious inclination to seek out only information that confirms what we believe we know and forces us to consider opposing viewpoints.

"You're not entitled to take a view, unless and until you can argue better against that view than the smartest guy who holds that opposite view. If you can argue better than the smartest person who holds the opposite view, that is when you are entitled to hold a certain view."
– Charlie Munger

There is one very simple strategy that will increase intellectual capacity: bursting one's filter bubble. Because filter bubbles operate in the subconscious, they often blind us to other viewpoints without our awareness. Bursting the filter bubble means intentionally seeking out people with different experiences and diametrically opposing perspectives. Simple... not easy.

Intellectual Humility

There's a well-known parable about six blind men who come upon an elephant and each experience it differently. One man feels the tail and says it's a rope, another feels the tusk and says it's a sword, and another contends it's a tree after feeling one of the elephant's legs, and so on the men go, each holding firm that his viewpoint is correct and the others are wrong. The moral of the story is that we tend to overestimate what we know and believe we are more correct than others when presented with a different viewpoint.

It's a prime example of illusory superiority bias, and it's true for politics, religion, social issues, and even fashion. At a time when it seems that we're all more convinced than ever of our own rightness, social scientists are exploring a concept called intellectual humility as a measure of one's ability to engage in civil discourse and learn from opposing viewpoints.

Imagine that two people are debating gun control; we can "see" their thoughts as we watch and listen to the exchange. One shares evidence from a gun expert about crime statistics. The other disputes that evidence as flawed or irrelevant. At the same time, his position that the evidence is flawed is driven more by his dislike of the person rather than by the evidence presented. That person is on the "other side," and so he's just wrong.

Think about the last time you fundamentally disagreed with someone about something important to you. You both had convictions, and maybe the conversation was more an attempt to convince the other to accept that information rather than a meaningful ideological exchange. We all enter such conversations on a broad spectrum of topics including politics, religion, parenting, gay rights, anything we feel very strongly about. Social scientists are exploring this concept called intellectual humility to determine how being firmly entrenched in "rightness" impacts ability to communicate, collaborate and learn with others.

Intellectual humility is recognizing intellectual limitations and not only being open to the possibility of being wrong, but also searching for new sources of evidence to disprove one's position. If intellectual humility is a mean between extremes, then closed-mindedness and intellectual arrogance would be on one side and insecurity or intellectual cowardice on the other.

Measuring intellectual humility has proven to be a challenge. As with measuring other personality traits, self-reports are an obvious choice and the most common tools, but, because intellectual humility is often perceived to be a socially desirable trait, people may be motivated to inflate their ratings. This tendency may be amplified by the *modesty effect*, which suggests that those who are truly intellectually humble will rate themselves lower while people who lack intellectual humility will rate themselves higher.

Some researchers believe that the best way to measure intellectual humility is through observations in certain kinds of interpersonal exchanges: conflict, praise, power struggle, or cultural differences among those who embrace different norms. Cognitive neuroscience may soon provide less subjective ways to measure intellectual humility. For example, recent studies report the use of EEGs to measure brain activity when subjects make errors or are engaged in challenging interpersonal situations.

Lazlo Bock, former senior VP of People Operations at Google, claims it was one of the most important qualities he looked for in a candidate. "Without intellectual humility, you are incapable of learning," Bock said. Psychologists agree with Bock, and a growing number of HR executives are incorporating intellectual humility into their requisite qualifications for new hires. New research shows that people with intellectual humility are better learners and collaborators because they don't disregard viewpoints that are different. Intellectual humility is also shown to correlate with higher levels of empathy, gratitude, altruism, benevolence, and lower levels of power seeking, all contributing factors to a healthy workplace environment.

In a 2017 study conducted at Duke University, researcher Mark Leary and his colleagues conducted a series of studies illustrating that intellectual humility increases tolerance, improves decision-making, and impacts the kinds of judgments we make about others.

One study showed that those with higher intellectual humility demonstrated a greater ability to learn new skills and comprehend new ideas. The second study looked at intellectual humility in terms of religious beliefs. Participants high in intellectual humility were less judgmental about the religious opinions of others. Another study examining political views found that participants high in intellectual humility were more inclined to see politicians who changed their attitudes as open-minded rather than "flip-floppers," and they were better able to engage in civil discourse with people who opposed their viewpoints.

However, having the willingness to not only listen to someone with an opposing viewpoint but also being able to learn from that person can be especially difficult when the topic involves deeply held beliefs. In 2016 *New York Magazine* partnered with a nonprofit organization to produce a documentary titled *Guns and Empathy*. The concept was a social experiment designed to examine whether gun victims and gun advocates could find a way to understand each other.

For three days, participants were paired with someone of an opposing view, each taking turns sharing and listening to the other's personal experiences. Afterward, participants were asked to put themselves in the shoes of the other person and reenact their partner's experience in front of the entire group. The results of the experiment were mixed. Some people acknowledged a new sense of empathy and understanding for those who held opposing views. They reported greater understanding of different perspectives on the issue; however, none of the participants changed their positions by the end of the study. Researchers concluded that empathy is very different from intellectual humility.

Intellectual humility is just as important in business as it is in politics and religion. People who are able to work together on teams with an openness for alternative perspectives are much more productive than teams comprised of members firmly entrenched in their own views. Leaders who exhibit low intellectual humility aren't open to new ideas and may even become defensive or hostile when their ideas are challenged. This not only dilutes the quality of ideas, but it sends a very strong message to team members about their ability to contribute. Great leaders are not only willing to hear perspectives that may be very different from their own, they also seek them out.

When focused on listening to opposing views rather than convincing someone of our own, we can use what we hear to make interactions more civil, more meaningful, and more productive. While our understanding of intellectual humility has expanded considerably over the last decade, this field of research is in its infancy. Much more remains to be learned. Until then, there is no debate that the world today could use a little more civil discourse. Perhaps a little more intellectual humility is the first step.

The Gap Between Perception and Reality

We'd all like to believe that the rational engine drives our thoughts, decisions, and behaviors. In reality, rationality takes work, and the brain is a bustling hub of activity. It looks for efficiencies to streamline the workload and is quite comfortable running on feeling and intuition. These efficiencies often turn the rational logic of the "if-then" principle into the irrational "if-then-I know" principle.

One could argue that "if-then-I know" logic is what has allowed us to survive and evolve. For example, a touch to a hot stove results in being burned and a quick jerk of the hand away. This "if-then-I know" statement is logical: If I touch a hot stove and then get burned, I know that touching a hot stove will burn me. All of the brain structures work the way they are supposed to, the rational brain wins, and the species survives another day. But that same logic doesn't apply to every experience. Consider these workplace examples where irrational conclusions create perceptions that are much different from reality:

Jan sent a proposal for a new product line to her boss a week ago. Her boss has been in a bad mood all week, but she hasn't mentioned the proposal.

Jan's "if-then-I know" statement: If I send a proposal to my boss, and she doesn't say anything about it and is in a bad mood, I know she hates the proposal.

Reality: Jan's boss hasn't even read the proposal yet because she's having angst about letting two team members go due to budget cuts.

Jim asked his boss for a meeting to get feedback on a project. They scheduled the meeting for the first thing Monday morning. Jim conscientiously prepared for the meeting over the weekend, only to have his boss cancel right before the scheduled time without explanation.

Jim's "if-then-I know" statement: If I schedule a meeting with my boss and then he suddenly cancels, I know he doesn't think what I do matters or that my work is important.

Reality: Jim's boss was in a fender bender on the way to work, and he knew he wouldn't make it to the meeting on time. He quickly canceled the meeting, however, to wait for the police.

These examples are common misperceptions, the kind we form all the time without even realizing it. In each scenario, the assumption is that the person has the necessary information to form a conclusion. In fact, that is seldom the case. The human brain looks for patterns and tries to identify them even when they are not there, just as illogical "if-then-I know" thinking often prompts us to jump to irrational conclusions. This process applies to every experience we interpret. When there is a gap between perception and reality, it is usually attributable to one or more of four factors: inadequate or inaccurate information, ineffective communication, skewed mental models, or unconscious biases.

All of these can lead to irrational thinking, judgments, decisions, and behavior. Everything we experience is influenced by countless factors that shape, color, or even distort those mental models and our perception of reality.

"It's not that I'm so smart.
It's just that I stay
with problems longer."

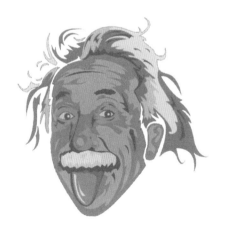

Got Grit?

Carol Dweck's research established that a growth mindset contributes to increased motivation, higher goals, and greater success. A person's attitude toward failure is essential to success in that those who can't effectively embrace and respond to failure are more likely to stay in the safety zone where mediocrity abounds.

Psychology professor at the University of Pennsylvania, Angela Duckworth, drills down a bit deeper. She studies non-IQ competencies to predict academic and professional success and takes her research beyond mindset. Drawing on her childhood experiences as the daughter of a scientist who frequently pointed out her "lack of genius," she maintains that the secret to success is a special combination of passion and persistence that she calls "grit."

Duckworth has explored this concept of grit with teachers in some of the toughest schools, finalists in the National Spelling Bee, and countless high achievers in virtually every sector of the business world. She found that the point of differentiation among high performers is how they process frustration and disappointment. High performers are conditioned to believe that obstacles and struggles are not cause for alarm, whereas lower performers are much more likely to panic and give up.

In 2004, she tested her grit theory with the West Point cadets at the United States Military Academy. At the time, West Point had initiated a comprehensive research project to predict accurately which cadets would make it through the grueling first phase known as "Beast Barracks" and which would pack up and go home. The study involved an exhaustive comparison of IQ, SAT and ACT scores, high school rank, physical fitness, "leadership potential," and additional tests that could be measured. Military psychologists even tried to discover subconscious similarities by showing the cadets flash cards of random images to determine the "it" factor among those who successfully made it through the program.

After all of the number crunching, the epiphanic moment came when one additional test was added, the Grit Test developed by Angela Duckworth. This test consists of 12 statements such as "I finish whatever I start" and "New ideas and projects sometimes distract me from previous ones." Of the 1,218 new cadets, 71 were defeated by the Beast Barracks. Those 71 cadets performed as well as their peers on every single test except the Grit Test. With statistical significance, West Point could now predict whether a cadet would complete the program or bail based upon this level of grittiness.

Perhaps the most essential attribute of gritty people is passion. Passion enables us to develop stamina and tenacity toward a higher purpose. This symbiosis creates meaning from chaos, finds value in effort, and cultivates happiness, personal satisfaction, and the sense that what we do really matters. People who genuinely love their work are motivated by their passion and a greater purpose. They tend to be happier, healthier, and more successful. Conversely, people who are unsatisfied with their work are also more likely to be dissatisfied with their personal relationships and experience distress in other areas of their lives.

"Nothing happens without desire and passion. Without it, nothing else falls in place. It's very hard to find someone who's successful and dislikes what they do."
–Malcolm Gladwell

Duckworth argues that grit is not only an underrated trait in our formative years and young adulthood but is also essential for professional success. She maintains that when we better understand disappointments and setbacks, we can then identify our beliefs about them and how those beliefs influence our behavior. "If people can change their beliefs about how success happens, then it is possible to change their behavior."

Persistence is the other essential ingredient in Duckworth's grit recipe. Defined as a firm course of action in spite of difficulty or opposition, gritty people understand that life can be messy and complicated and often situations do not have easy answers. Persistence requires planning, preparation, and continued work toward the goal.

Resilience is also necessary as it gives us the confidence to experiment when the inevitable orange cones of life present unplanned detours and uncertain paths.

As Andrew Zolli and Ann Marie Healy point out in their book, *Resilience: Why Things Bounce Back,* "There are no finish lines and no silver bullets to success. It must be continually refreshed." Resilience is the difference between those who thrive and those who fall apart in uncertain or challenging times.

In a 2013 interview with *Entrepreneur* magazine, Zolli said, *"There are many determinants of personal resilience, like the strength of your social networks, the quality of your intimate relationships, your genes, your life experiences, your physical health, your access to resources. If you believe the world is a meaningful place, and you have agency in your life, and believe successes and failures are put in place to teach, rather than just being horrible accidents, resilience emerges in the face of disruption when it occurs."*

Extensive research confirms that successful people share common attitudes about challenges and opportunities for growth. Here, however, is the bottom line: Frustration and failure often come as a package deal and while neither feels good, both are essential to stretching and growing and succeeding. Courage and grit are a package deal, too. The most successful people aren't afraid to fail, and they don't let frustration defeat them. They've discovered the power of vulnerability.

Critics, Courage, and Convictions

"Bob" is a friend and colleague I worked with years ago. At one point, the company went through a major reorganization, several divisions were dissolved, and Bob was one of many employees whose position was eliminated. Bob was one of the most conscientious employees I knew in that company. He was smart, dedicated, talented, and passionate about his work. He was 60-something at the time, too young to retire, and, in his opinion, too old to start over. The economy tanked, jobs were scarce, and Bob was scared. He hasn't worked since.

He and I still stay in touch and chat from time to time. I'll ask him what he's been up to, and the answer is always the same, "Still shuffling along." He might share a good book that he's read or an update on a mutual friend, but other than that, he's just shuffling along. The last time we spoke, he was more despondent than ever. After reminiscing a bit about the old times, he quietly said, "You know, when that chapter ended, I felt so scared and vulnerable. I don't feel that way anymore. I guess don't feel much anymore."

After the call, I couldn't get his words out of my head. Bob's fear of failure kept him trapped in a state of apathy, paralyzed by his own insecurities. "...scared and vulnerable..." All of that talent, intellect, and passion were thwarted by a lack of courage and conviction to face his inner critic. He wasn't vulnerable; he was defeated by his inability to be vulnerable.

Embracing a challenge at the risk of failure certainly requires a growth mindset, grit, intellectual humility, and perseverance. But, the other essential ingredient is vulnerability. It's far easier to persevere and take risks within one's comfort zone. Confidence fuels persistence.

Still, taking those risks when we lack confidence for the world to see increases the stakes with a far greater chance of getting criticized, rejected, or hurt by others. Whether it's a new job, an important meeting, the creative process, or a struggling friendship, the biggest critic often lives inside us, fueling our fears. It takes courage and conviction to overcome our insecurities and be vulnerable.

People often use the words *vulnerability* and *insecurity* interchangeably. But there is an important distinction. Insecurity implies weakness, uncertainty, and the need for protection. It can become a debilitating obsession of one's limitations. While vulnerability is often grounded in uncertainty, risk, and emotional exposure, it is the genesis of intimacy, genuine connections, and creativity. It isn't the experience that causes harm or results in reward; it's the response to that experience that determines the outcome.

"Vulnerability is not winning or losing; it's having the courage to show up and be seen when we have no control over the outcome. Vulnerability is not weakness; it's our greatest measure of courage," affirms research professor and author Brené Brown in her book, *Rising Strong: How the*

Ability to Reset Transform the Way We Live, Love, Parent and Lead.

Brown has worked with people across a wide range of professions such as Fortune 500 leaders, artists, teachers, parents, even couples in long-term relationships. Much of her research has focused on determining why some people have the ability to find the courage required to get back up after falling. The focus of her research examined essence of grit. She asked, "What do these people with strong and loving relationships, leaders nurturing creativity, artists pushing innovation, and clergy walking with people through faith and mystery have in common?" The answer was clear: They recognize the power of vulnerability and they're not afraid to get a little uncomfortable.

Living a brave life is not always easy. We all face personal and professional challenges that start out scary. The "what ifs" get louder. What if I can't...? What if I don't...? What if I won't...? And, we are all, inevitably, going to stumble and fall at times. But, often the visions of failure, judgment, and ridicule are far worse in one's head than the actual fall. It's that inner critic that reminds us of more defeats than victories. The inner critic, fueled by fear, convinces us that losing will hurt more than winning will feel good. The brain has a way of tricking us that way. The inner critic isn't all bad, though. It's this conflict between fear and conviction that is the impetus for a sense of vulnerability empowered by courage.

Think of vulnerability, fear, courage, and conviction as relatives discussing a challenge. Fear immediately zooms into the risk of criticism, rejection, or failure screaming, "Abort! Abort!" Fear has always been closed-minded and impulsive and even bossy at times. Vulnerability and fear have spent a lot of time together in stressful situations, and vulnerability knows fear well enough to expect this reaction.

Vulnerability initially listens to fear and contemplates the threat of exposure and the inner critic's condemnation. Vulnerability knows from past experience that fear tends to have a myopic perspective. Vulnerability has learned the value of consulting courage and his brother, conviction, to see the big picture. They're able to recognize meaningful human connections, innovation, and opportunities to stretch and grow. Vulnerability can let fear win, or it can let courage and conviction chart a different course. As part of the family, fear might tag along, but when courage and conviction lead the way, vulnerability puts fear in its proper place: "I see you. I hear you. And I'm doing this anyway."

Courage doesn't mean there is no fear. Courage is the measure of how much your fears challenge your convictions. Ultimately, if we are fortunate, we realize that the real reward comes from being vulnerable and naked, not despite it. It's the difference between people who step out of their comfort zones to stretch and grow and those who are imprisoned within their comfort zones.

Striving for progress doesn't mean striving for perfection. Mistakes are inevitable. Ultimately, our convictions bring those mistakes to light and transform them into the source of learning, change, and growth. Convictions are the guiding force behind doing the next right thing when we falter. Perhaps there is nothing more empowering than the sense of agency that emerges when one recognizes that the power of vulnerability lies in the admission of humanity, imperfections and all.

"Owning our story can be hard but not nearly as difficult as spending our lives running from it. Embracing our vulnerabilities is risky but not nearly as dangerous as giving up on love and belonging and joy – the experiences that make us the most vulnerable. Only when we are brave enough to explore the darkness will we discover the infinite power of our light."
-Brené Brown

"If you want to live a happier life,
tie it to a goal,
not to people or objects."

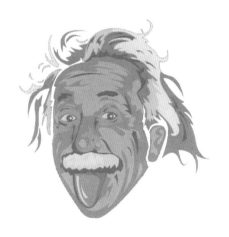

Setting Goals, Reaching Goals

Back in 1976, a young man named Jerry graduated from Queens College with a degree in communications; his dream, however, was to become a comedian. To that purpose, he started writing jokes and performing at local comedy clubs. On a good night, he might make $50, but most of the time, he didn't get paid. He longed for the day he would make it big but would spend the next four years supporting himself with menial jobs.

As a tele-marketer, he made cold calls to sell lightbulbs. He also waited tables, did custodial work, and sold costume jewelry from a street cart. He was broke and discouraged, but he kept working local clubs.

One night, a casting agent caught his act and offered him an opportunity to audition for a new sitcom called Benson. Ironically, he got the part of a mail delivery kid named Frankie, an aspiring comedian who wasn't very funny. After three episodes, however, he showed up for a read-through only to learn that he'd been fired.

Never again, he vowed. Though he was humiliated, he went right back to comedy. He knew if he was going to make it, he needed to write better jokes. The best way to do that was to write more jokes. He set a goal to write jokes every single day for a year.

To stay motivated and committed to his goal, he hung a 12-month banner calendar on the wall so he could see the entire year at once. Each day that he wrote, he put a big red X on that day of the calendar. A few days in a row turned into a whole week and then a whole month. The more Xs he put on the calendar, the more motivated he became not to break the streak. Before long, he looked forward to putting that big red X on the calendar every day. Writing was no longer a chore to put off; it was a welcome part of his routine.

That guy was Jerry Seinfeld. According to *Forbes* magazine, Seinfeld made $267 million in 1998. A decade later, he was still averaging about $85 million per year. Today, he is listed as one of the "Top 100 Comedians of All-Time" by Comedy Central. No one can challenge Seinfeld's success.

What's the secret to his success? Some would argue he'd never have been that successful without talent, while others might attribute his success to grit and tenacity. Either way, setting a huge goal and then taking even one step toward that goal every single day is easier said than done. As it turns out, there is science behind Seinfeld's strategy for success. There is also is a wealth of research illuminating neuroscientific discoveries about goals, motivation, and behavior change.

The formal definition of a goal is "a desired future state or outcome coupled with a set of steps or acts that promote the attainment of that future state or outcome." Put more simply, a goal is something desired but not obtainable without some intervention, motivation, or behavior change. It's a deviation from the path of least resistance. Effective goal-setting is about changing habits or creating a new routine, and the brain hates change. Goals that require a significant change in thinking or behavior will automatically be resisted. From a neurological perspective, the success or failure of any goal involves four basic processes: the reticular activating system, the dopamine loop, the power of procrastination, and cognitive bias.

Reticular Activating System

Have you ever discovered a television series or movie you've never heard of before and then begin to notice it everywhere? Perhaps after considering the purchase of a new car, you suddenly see a million of them on the road. Maybe you've experienced hearing someone call your name in a crowded room full of people. Enter the reticular activating system, or RAS, hard at work. The RAS is a small neural region at the top of the spinal column. All senses except smell, which goes to our brain's emotional center, are wired directly to this small bundle of neurons.

While it may be small, it has a huge job. The RAS is the brain's bouncer or the informational gate-keeper. It decides what information to let in and what information to toss out. Think about the immense amount of the visual stimuli around us. Scientists estimate that the conscious mind can handle about 100 pieces of information every second. The human eye captures more than 300 megapixels of visual information every second.

Most of this information never makes it to conscious awareness before the RAS bouncer kicks it out. Imagine how overwhelmed the brain would be if it had to process all of the incoming sensory stimuli in the environment! The RAS determines what is relevant and what is just clutter.

The RAS also plays a vital role in motivation and goal-setting. Often, the biggest obstacle to reaching a goal is staying focused and motivated long enough. Research in goal-setting and motivation maintains that the RAS activates our arousal system by keeping the relevant information at the top of the mind and filtering out other information irrelevant to the goal. When setting a goal, the RAS is automatically in motion, paying attention to the positive people, activities, or things that will enable us to actualize on those goals.

Dopamine Feedback Loop

Those who post on a social media site or write a blog post tend to monitor the post like a hawk to see how many likes, comments, shares, hearts, and smiley faces it has garnered. The more the interaction, the more they check the progress. They are the victims of a dopamine feedback loop, and the hearts, likes, comments, and shares give them a buzz. They are also signals to the brain to release dopamine.

Dopamine is best known for the role it plays in addiction and drug use. Its presence enables us to feel pleasure and enjoyment from food, sex, drugs, gambling, alcohol, whatever the source of addiction. It is also the "seeking" chemical. Think of it as the "I did it drug." It is released from the limbic system when we feel the rush of success. It's also the drug that says, "Ooohh... that felt good. Do that again!" Though its presence is what makes addiction so tough to overcome, it can be just as powerful as a driver toward reaching a goal. The dopamine response does not last long, but when we remember how good that thing felt, those intensely pleasurable feelings make us want to get it again.

Such repetition leads to the dopamine feedback loop, which can be good or bad depending upon the source of pleasure. After repeated experiences, the dopamine boost gets smaller, and the level of pleasure decreases. For the addict, more of the drug is necessary to get the same high. For the goal seeker, motivation to reach the goal is enhanced. the same goals, however, week after week will eventually weaken the dopamine rush. To get the same buzz, bigger targets must be set, bigger challenges tackled, or bigger risks taken.

Not only do we want the rush again and need a more significant experience to get it, but we also begin to anticipate the sensation. The dopamine feedback loop is sensitive to cues that signal more pleasure. When a trigger indicates we'll get another rush, the dopamine system is set in motion. Ultimately, it's not the actual reward that perpetuates the loop; it's the anticipation of the reward.

The Power of Procrastination

We all procrastinate sometimes. Recent studies indicate that procrastination isn't just bad for our goals; it also impacts our health. Putting off important tasks makes us feel guilty, and that guilt increases stress, which contributes to a host of health issues such as poor sleep habits, higher anxiety and depression, and lower immunity. Research maintains that the 20% of people who are chronic procrastinators are also more prone to cardiovascular disease and hypertension than others.

What is the procrastinator's most common excuse? Time! There is never enough time in the day! The thing about time, though, is that it's one of the few resources dealt to all in the same amount of 24 hours, every single day. Some people spend those hours doing amazing things, each a step toward the finish line. Other people bounce between distractions that keep those goals just out of reach.

Newsflash: Soon is not a time and someday is not a plan.

Procrastination isn't a new concept, as it dates back to Aristotle and Socrates. It was referred to as *akrasia,* which, according to the Oxford Dictionary, is defined as "the state of mind in which someone acts against their better judgment through weakness of will."

Thousands of years later, we know that weakness of will is the result of a tug of war for control inside the brain. It's a battle between the limbic system and the prefrontal cortex. The limbic system, also known as the instant-gratification seeker, lives in the now and loves pleasure and reward. The prefrontal cortex is the rational decision maker that can visualize the future and plan, reason, and then take steps to reach goals. What makes things a little tricky is that because the limbic system is designed in part to keep us alive, it's dominant and automatic. There's nothing automatic, however, about the prefrontal cortex, the rational decision maker. The activity here is conscious and intentional. When one's focus drifts away from intentional thought, the limbic system sees the opening and jumps back in to take over again.

The instant-gratification seeker is responsible for what psychologists call *present bias* or the urgency effect. Being instantly gratified merely means that we tend to value immediate rewards or payoffs that are closer to the present time than those further in the future. The further into the future the reward lies, the less value we put on it, even when the value is the same.

For example, if offered $100 in 9 months or $150 in 12 months, the rational decision maker would step in and reason, "If I can wait nine months, then I can wait a little longer for the extra money." If, however, the choice were

$100 now and $150 in a year, the instant-gratification seeker would most likely take the $100 and run. Both options present the same reward: $100 sooner or $150 later. If choosing the $100 now, then why not choose it in nine months? Present bias skews our perception of value based upon time.

Other studies suggest that present bias doesn't just skew our perception of value; it also skews our perception of "self." Hal Hershfield, a psychologist at UCLA Anderson School of Management, has studied this construct of present and future self. He looked at fMRI scans of brain activity as subjects thought about themselves in three different states: themselves in the here and now, as a celebrity like Matt Damon or Natalie Portman, and themselves in the future.

He found that people process information about their present and future selves with different parts of the brain. More significant, brain activity when describing the future self was similar to brain activity when describing celebrities. Even though intellectually we know that the present self is the same person as the future self, we treat that future self as a different person who doesn't share the benefits or consequences of present actions.

Hershfield took his research even further to determine if it is possible to reduce present bias by actually seeing the future self. He divided the subjects into two groups. One group viewed photos that were digitally altered to create a realistically aged version of the participants. Then, all of the subjects were hypothetically given $1,000 and asked how much they wanted to set aside for their retirement. Those who saw the image of their future selves consistently allocated twice as much as those who didn't. Those who didn't view the digitally altered photos were able to separate the future self from the present self as if they weren't responsible for that "other person."

Visceral States

George Loewenstein conducted a famous study published in the *Journal of Organizational Behavior and Human Decision-Making Processes* exploring visceral states. Loewenstein makes the argument that visceral states such as hunger, exhaustion, sexual desire, and intense emotions cause people to behave contrary to their own long-term goals and self-interest even with full awareness that they are doing so. He likens the power of visceral factors to a relapse with drug addiction. Relapse is always preceded by a decision to use again even when the addict knows it is a bad and many times fatal course of action. It is an impulsive decision, not a rational one, provoked by an intense and overwhelming craving.

It's not just the drug addict who makes impulsive decisions based upon visceral factors. High-pressure salespersons, realtors, and other professionals manipulate emotions when they use the "power of now." *This house won't be on the market long... make an offer before someone else does... limited editions... one-time-only deal.* These "suggestions" are all designed to create a sense of urgency and action.

Loewenstein maintains that the intensity of a visceral state, a craving, hunger, exhaustion, or a strong emotional feeling can drive a wedge between behavior and our perceived self-interest. We can realign our self-interest with our behavior when we learn to identify the visceral factors we feel in the moment and understand that they subside over time. Understanding how emotions and natural and subconscious tendencies like the urgency effect and present-bias work can help prevent impulsive decision-making and keep us moving toward our goals.

The key to achieving any big goal is to take reasonable steps intentionally and consistently toward it. Break the task or project down into smaller chunks. If you want to write a book, commit to writing one page every day. Once you get into it, you'll likely find yourself writing more. Here are a few more simple ways to outsmart your instant-gratification seeker:

See the progress.
Seeing an accomplishment is a reward in itself. It's the brain's way of tricking the limbic system into thinking it has won while the prefrontal cortex continues to focus on the task. Put a glass jar on the desk and add a paperclip or a marble every time progress toward the goal is made. Or, print the calendar and highlight tasks completed as each is done. It sounds simple, but just like Jerry Seinfeld's calendar, visually seeing tasks done right before your eyes will release enough dopamine to keep you motivated in pursuit of your goal.

Redefine the rewards.
Amelia Earhart once said, "The most difficult thing is the decision to act. The rest is merely tenacity. The fears are paper tigers. You can do anything you decide to do. You can act to change and control your life and the procedure. The process is its own reward." Learn how to find rewards in the process, marking days on the calendar with an X or adding marbles to a jar, and celebrate the journey as well as the destination.

Find an accountability partner.
The best way to stay committed to anything is to ask someone you trust to help keep you honest. If it is someone who shares your goal, then you're helping each other. Agree to provide updates such as a quick text, a phone call, or maybe a regular coffee date once a week. Not only will it be easier to stick to your goal, but you'll get the added bonus of feeling connected with someone in a meaningful way.

Eat the frog.
Mark Twain once said, "Eat a live frog first thing in the morning and nothing worse will happen to you the rest of the day." Identify your frog, that thing that looms large and scary or consider the most important task on your list. Even if you know you won't finish it, starting your day with it makes it a little smaller and a little less scary.

"If we trace out what we behold and experience through the language of logic, we are doing science; if we show it in forms whose interrelationships are not accessible to our conscious thought but intuitively recognized as meaningful, we are doing art."

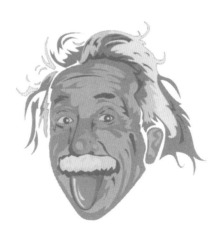

Mental Shortcuts to Irrationality

Are you a rational person? Do you think of yourself as someone who doesn't jump to conclusions but rather as one who chooses actions based upon facts, evidence, experience, or well-reasoned arguments? We all like to think we have control over our decisions, judgments, and perceptions of the world. In reality, though, such control does not exist. A wealth of psychology and cognitive-science research tells us the brain is complex and amazing, yet also fickle and lazy. This complex part of us is easily influenced by unconscious patterns of thoughts or mental shortcuts that impact the way we perceive and interact with the world.

Consider the following scenario: You schedule a meeting with a client at 3:00 at a coffee shop across town. Your day is crazy, you're putting out fires left and right, traffic is nuts, and it feels as if you're moving mountains to be there on time. You consider texting him to push the meeting by 15 minutes but dismiss it and race to the meeting. At 2:59 you pull into the parking lot, tires screeching, and sprint through the door. You look around but don't see him, so you catch your breath and grab a cup of coffee. Fourteen minutes later, he texts you: "running late... be there in 10." While it so easily could have been you late for many "reasons beyond your control," you made it on time, and he didn't, and you're irritated.

Let's face it... we're human. Things happen. We've all been on both sides of such a scenario. The interesting thing is the variance between our perspective as the *disrespector* and the *disrespectee*. Think about the last time you were late for an appointment. The traffic was horrible, your prior meeting ran long, you couldn't find a parking spot. When we fall short, we usually have "reasons." But when someone else falls short, we instinctually perceive it as a faulty character trait: *That person is rude... he doesn't respect my time... she can't manage her time.*

Behavioral scientists refer to this as *fundamental attribution error.* Also known as correspondence bias, it's the tendency to place greater emphasis on situational factors when considering our own behavior while putting greater emphasis on character or intention when considering the behavior of others. This bias is just one example of the mental shortcuts or cognitive biases that result in irrational behavior, and we all have them.

What is Cognitive Bias?

A cognitive bias is a systematic deviation from rational judgment that often leads to perceptual distortion, inaccurate judgment, illogical interpretation, or what is broadly referred to as irrationality. In simpler terms, such bias is how the brain has evolved to manage huge amounts of incoming data and stimuli efficiently, allocate cognitive resources, and compensate for limited processing ability.

Such unconscious drivers influence judgment and decision-making for all of us. Sometimes, they help us make faster decisions when time is more important than accuracy. Other times, these short-cuts are "by-products" of human processing limitations resulting from what psychologists refer to as *bounded rationality*, the inclination to seek a satisfactory solution rather than an optimal one.

Cognitive biases arise from a variety of mental processes including:

- Information-processing overload
- Mental "noise" (memory deficiencies)
- Emotional and moral motivations
- Social influence

Whatever the cause, more often than not, biases prevent us from making sound, reasoned judgments, and such biases kick in without our even realizing it. Because our brains are wired to process information as quickly and efficiently as possible, we are not very good at recognizing our own biases. The tendency to see ourselves as less biased than others is known as our cognitive blind spot, and just as we all have biases, we also all have a cognitive blind spot.

Seeing is Believing

Unconscious bias has been identified, observed, and validated in brain studies using Magnetic Resonance Imaging (MRI) technology, and its existence is now acknowledged by psychologists and neuroscientists as real and measurable. Studies conducted at Harvard University using the Harvard Implicit Association Test have revealed that decision-making automatically triggers specific regions of the brain responsible for unconscious processing. These scans show that activity increases in the amygdala (the region responsible for processing emotions, specifically fear) when the brain responds to perceived threats. We automatically create biases, or mental shortcuts, as survival mechanisms.

Mathew Dylan Lieberman, a professor and Social Cognitive and Neuroscience Lab director at UCLA, uses functional neuroimaging and neuropsychology to explore unconscious processes. He explains:

"Unconscious cognition is essential to human functioning; it helps us to be efficient and responsive to the world around us. However, unconscious processes are also prone to errors that remain unrecognized and uncorrected, which can lead to flawed decision-making, significant bias, and blinkered thinking." (Matthew Lieberman, 2014)

An evolving list of almost 200 biases has emerged over the last 50 years and continues to grow. This body of research on human judgment and decision-making expands on a regular basis in cognitive science, social psychology, and behavioral economics. Many of these findings can inform and improve the way we think, learn, communicate, and collaborate in and out of the workplace.

The Father of Irrational Behavior

One of the leading experts on cognitive bias is psychologist, Princeton professor, author, and Nobel Prize-winning economist Daniel Kahneman. If those credentials aren't impressive enough, *The Economist* listed him as the seventh most influential economist on the planet in 2015. Kahneman challenges the assumption of human rationality and maintains that quirks, logical inconsistencies, and flaws in decision-making represent the rule rather than the exception in cognitive processing.

He has devoted his career to studying the heuristics and biases that explain how people make judgments that impact decisions as well as the conditions under which these decisions are unreliable and irrational. A *heuristic* is defined as an approach to a problem or decision that is not guaranteed to be a perfect solution but merely a "sufficient one." Some examples of heuristic shortcuts that ease the cognitive load are intuition, trial and error, educated guesses, and using the rule of thumb.

As Daniel Kahneman explains in his book, *Thinking, Fast and Slow*, we rely on two parallel systems when we make decisions. "System 1" is the system of expedience, the system used to make decisions based on what comes to mind very quickly or what just "feels right." Such intuitive reactions and instantaneous decisions are made all the time. Some examples of System 1 tasks include:

- Stopping at a stop sign
- Reading the text on a billboard
- Understanding simple sentences
- Using a credit card to pay for gas

System 2 is slower and more difficult to engage, requiring more cognitive effort and concentration. This deliberate type of thinking involves analysis, reasoning, self-control, or demanding physical tasks. Some examples of System 2 tasks include:

- Remembering a phone number
- Declining chocolate cake to stay on a diet
- Deciding which car to buy
- Looking for a friend in a crowded room

Kahneman classifies decisions made into these two systems and explores biases and irrational decision-making associated with each. For example, because System 1 decisions are made so quickly, the brain is required to take shortcuts that work to an advantage such as the reflexive decision to swerve to avoid an accident with an oncoming car. When shortcuts are taken in System 2 tasks, important details may be overlooked or objectivity sacrificed. System 2 kicks in when System 1's mistakes must be corrected; however, when the brain is actively engaged in a System 2 activity, System 1 has greater influence over behavior.

Numerous studies have explored this transfer of power between systems. For example, imagine the need to remember a phone number without writing it down. While focusing on the number and repeating it mentally, a snack is offered, either healthy vegetables and hummus or a not-so-healthy decadent chocolate dessert. Research suggests that when System 2 is busy remembering the numbers, one has less self-control and is likely to choose the dessert with very little thought. System 1 puts that chocolate in the mouth before an unsuspecting soul can say, "I'll resume my diet tomorrow."

Kahneman's work also shows that when the brain is occupied with System 2 thinking, it interferes with any other type of System 2 thinking needed to be performed at the same time. In addition, when engaged in one type of System 2 thinking, we are less able to perform another System 2 immediately afterward, even if these are two different types of activities (i.e., physical, cognitive, or emotional). It seems best, then, never to schedule back-to-back meetings requiring a high level of intellectual acuity. It's also why scheduling a 15-minute break after 45 minutes of concentrated focus fosters greater productivity.

Proxies of Expertise

In addition to understanding how individual biases lead to flawed individual decisions, researchers have also been exploring how these biases influence group dynamics. One of the most important assets a group can have is the expertise of its members, but studies show that we often subconsciously fall prey to proxies of expertise, a phrase coined by University of Utah professor Bryan Bonner. Bonner found that instead of giving the most credence to the people with actual expertise, we have a natural tendency to pay attention to the person who talks often or loudly, has the most impressive title, or shares a common interest.

The three biases that trick a person into falling for proxies of expertise are similarity, experience, and expedience. Similarity bias is the unconscious preference for "people like me" over "people not like me." Experience bias refers to the confidence that our perceptions are accurate. It's a natural tendency to assume we have all the information we need to form an opinion and our opinions are more accurate than the opinions of others. Expedience bias results in making quick decisions based on intuition or a gut feeling rather than taking the time to research, search for potential flaws or explore other alternatives.

These shortcuts lead to inaccurate judgments of people based upon irrelevant factors rather than on skill or intellect. Research shows that even when all members of a group recognize one person as an expert on a given subject, they often give more credence to someone else based upon illogical and irrational factors.

Some studies show that the ideas of the loudest or most talkative are considered with more weight than others. Other studies show that taller people have an advantage in groups over those with less-prominent statures, and members subconsciously favor others with whom they share common interests over those with whom they don't. These proxies of expertise impact who contributes to the group and whose ideas are considered. Inevitably, this approach often leads to the exclusion of some very smart people.

When people aren't given opportunities to contribute their strengths, they either quit and leave, or they quit and stay.

Bias at Work in the Workplace

In the workplace, unconscious biases can influence everything from who gets hired or fired to collaboration and group decision-making to team success. Every day in any organization, people make decisions, interact with colleagues, manage people, or take some kind of action based upon unconscious conclusions, beliefs, or perceptions. These unconscious cognitive processes often result in costly mistakes and miscalculations, poor employee engagement, and dysfunctional team dynamics, all of which impact company culture and bottom line.

The first step in addressing unconscious biases in the workplace is acknowledging that we all have them. These biases are not faults or weaknesses but rather cognitive functions we cannot completely control. Knowing what they are and recognizing them when they happen will help prevent them from sabotaging team efforts and undermining organizational success.

Consider these common biases that may be hard at work sabotaging teams.

Confirmation Bias

The brain loves to be right. Confirmation bias is the tendency to seek out evidence that proves that what we already believe to be true is true while ignoring contradicting evidence, even if such evidence is factual and valid. It explains why it seems impossible to persuade someone arguing for or against a hot topic issue such as pro-life/pro-choice or gun control to consider the merits of the opposite stance. Confirmation bias is one of the most common biases that subconsciously influence everyday decisions in the workplace. For example, suppose a team is tasked with determining which division should launch the next new product. Some think it should be a summer learning program for the education division, but the research indicates that the market is saturated with more-established and trusted brands.

Confirmation bias prevents thinkers from accepting the conflicting data, conducting more extensive market research to find an untapped niche, or even doing informal testing to prove that a preconception may not be the best move going forward. Combined with the optimism bias, confirmation bias reinforces that one position must be correct and underestimates any probability that it isn't. Many times, it leads down the wrong road.

Illusory Superiority and the Dunning-Kruger Effect

The illusory superiority bias is often at the core of conflicts in team tasks. Our natural inclination is to overestimate our own knowledge and skills. One of the first studies that identified illusory superiority was conducted by the College Board in 1976. More than a million students taking the SATs that year were given a survey asking how they ranked relative to the median of the sample (rather than the average peer) on a number of characteristics. In ratings of leadership abilities, 70% of the students self-reported above the median. In the ability to get along with others, 85% put themselves above the median; 25% rated themselves in the top 1%.

Research shows that most of us are very bad at assessing our own abilities and competencies, leading to a phenomenon called the Dunning-Kruger Effect. Nobel Prize winners David Dunning and Justin Kruger stated that "persons of low ability suffer from illusory superiority when they mistakenly assess their cognitive ability as greater than it is." Their research concludes that the less skilled one is, the less likely this person is to recognize this lack of skill. Furthermore, the least-competent performers inflate abilities the most.

Examples of the Dunning-Kruger Effect abound. One study discovered that 32-42% of software engineers rated their skills as being in the top 5% of their companies. A nationwide survey found that 21% of Americans believe that it's "very likely" or "fairly likely" that they'll become millionaires within the next 10 years.

The irony of the Dunning-Kruger Effect is that the knowledge and intelligence required to be good at a task are often the same qualities needed to recognize that one is not good at that task. Furthermore, in lacking that knowledge and intelligence, one remains ignorant that he or she is not good at that task. It's the epitome of someone who doesn't know what he doesn't know.

Affinity Bias or the Similarity Bias

The affinity bias is best described as the people-like-me bias, the natural tendency to align with people we share common interests or traits with. For example, if a friend enjoys talking about football with John in the breakroom, the similarity principle says that he is more likely to support, subconsciously, his ideas in a meeting than Dan's, a person with whom nothing in common is shared. It is a subconscious inclination to overlook the faults or mistakes of people we like and notice the faults and mistakes of those we don't, resulting in unfounded conclusions and poor decisions. Research shows that similarity is one of the biggest factors influencing hiring practices. Interviewers naturally have a stronger affinity towards people they like even though those who are different or not liked as much may have a much stronger skill set or be better qualified for the position. In addition, this similarity bias limits diversity. Diverse teams have a wide range of strengths, giving them an advantage in overcoming a wide spectrum of challenges.

Negativity Bias

Negativity bias is the natural tendency to place greater weight on negative thoughts, emotions, or social interactions than neutral or positive thoughts. When presented with a decision in which one can either gain or lose, the natural tendency is to consider the potential loss more than the potential gain. From an evolutionary standpoint, focusing on potential loss is what has prevented our extinction, a way we have evolved to survive. It's more important to be on the lookout for lions and tigers than to decide which berry is the tastiest. The brain has learned to fast-track danger to the amygdala and crank up the intensity to keep us alive.

Jonathan Haidt, social psychologist and author of *The Happiness Hypothesis: Finding Modern Truth in Ancient Wisdom*, explains this phenomenon as an "evolutionarily adaptation for bad to be stronger than good." He writes, "Responses to threats and unpleasantness are faster, stronger, and harder to inhibit than responses to opportunities and pleasures. The brain produces a greater surge in electrical activity when faced with negative stimuli than with positive or neutral stimuli and has evolved to react long before it realizes that to which it is reacting. As Ben Franklin said, 'We are not so sensible of the greatest Health as of the least Sickness.' "
Negativity bias explains why company culture and employee engagement are far more damaged by dissatisfaction, stress, or frustration than improved by Frisbee Fridays, team-building exercises or incentives.

Countless studies show that negative emotions diminish social and intellectual resources as well as individual and team performance.

One study conducted by Emily Heaphy and Marcial Losada analyzed 60 business teams to determine how positive and negative comments impacted team effectiveness. This effectiveness was measured by financial performance, customer satisfaction, and feedback from the team members. Results showed that the most influential factor impacting effectiveness was the ratio of positive to negative comments; this ratio of positive to negative comments on the highest performing teams was 5.6 to 1, and the ratio on the lowest performing teams was 1 to 3, three negative comments for every positive one!

Leaders who communicate negativity are even more impactful than team dynamics, partially because they inherently carry more influence and partially because employees jump to wondering if they have done something to cause it. If leaders feel stressed or angry, even if their negative emotions have nothing to do with the team, they will spread the negativity and induce cortisol production in those around them. Emotional contagion is real.

The bottom line is that scientific evidence proves that the brain and body operate better when a person is in a positive mental state. One practical way to overcome this bias is to practice "realistic optimism." Recognizing our tendency to look for the negatives and then intentionally shifting to focus on the positives broadens our scope of attention and cognition, enables us to tap into intellectual resources, and strengthens social relationships.

Survivorship Bias

Survivorship bias is the tendency to focus on survivors instead of "non-survivors," depending on the situation. In the workplace, focus is on winners instead of losers, on success stories rather than failures. This emphasis on successes is a dangerous practice.

For example, if asked to name successful entrepreneurs, Bill Gates, Richard Branson, Steve Jobs, Oprah Winfrey, or Mark Zuckerberg might come to mind. No doubt they are all successful. Emulating the superstars may seem intuitive. Remember, though, that all of these people could also all be described as risk-takers and rogue thinkers who kept going, even though people said they were nuts.

Risk-taking and going against the grain can lead to success, but they do not guarantee success. Not much is heard about those rogue thinkers who took big risks on the "whatever widget" that will revolutionize the way things are done and ended up in financial ruin. Maybe they did have the right widget but made a critical error in execution, leading to their demise. Knowledge of that piece of information could be the secret to success. Survivorship bias prevents using mistakes to an advantage. By only focusing on success, valuable learning and lessons are missed, and often the best ideas are buried in those lessons.

Anchoring Bias

Anchoring bias is the tendency to latch onto one piece of information and disregard other important facts or evidence when making decisions. Often, such a bias occurs with the first thing heard. One example of anchoring is frequently evident in negotiations. The first person to open a negotiation has significant control over the price range. Whatever number the initiator throws out is subconsciously and automatically planted as the anchor and is used to formulate a counteroffer. Leaders must be especially aware and wary of this bias.

Imagine a VP of sales meets with the team for a quarterly review of the numbers. By inquiring what the team thinks about cutting marketing efforts in one particular division by 25%, the team leader has planted that number as the anchor. Once that anchor is established, it's tough to build from anything but that. Brands use it all the time to get us to buy their products. For example, let's say the MSRP for a new car is $39,995. You negotiate the price down to $33,595 and get a travel mug, too. You believe you got a deal, and the anchoring effect worked.

Airtime Bias

Airtime is what scientists in the field refer to as the equality of conversational turn-taking. Researchers have found that how much someone talks is often more influential than that person's experience or qualifications. Qualities like confidence and extroversion outweigh knowledge or experience; therefore, influence is determined by who talks first, who talks the most, or who talks the loudest.

For example, typically the first few people to share ideas in a brainstorming session are those who are passionate about the project or feel they have the most to offer the group; think illusory superiority. These are not the introverts, as introverts are rarely the first to contribute to a discussion. They also may not be the most experienced. The airtime bias leads people to accept the views of the talkers, confusing quantity with quality. Meanwhile, some of the best ideas may be dismissed or overlooked simply due to airtime bias, a perfect reason for leaders to speak less, later, or last.

The Halo Effect

The halo effect is the inclination to form an overall impression of someone based upon a single attribute. The effect works in both positive and negative directions and is sometimes referred to as the horns and halo effect. If one aspect of a person is seen as negative, there is a subconscious natural tendency to have a negative predisposition toward unrelated characteristics. A classic example of the horns effect is judging an unattractive person as less qualified for a position than an attractive person with the same qualifications. This horns effect is also called discrimination!

The halo effect is especially prevalent in annual performance reviews. If an employee is competent in one area of her job, the natural tendency is to assume proficiency in other areas, even though supporting data may be lacking. Likewise, an employee who is incompetent in one or two aspects of his role may be labeled as incompetent across the board, again, without supporting data.

The horns and halo effect can play a significant role in group decision-making and team dynamics. For example, if a member of the team consistently makes minor mistakes on day-to-day tasks, the group may disregard any ideas offered by that person in brainstorming sessions. The converse would also apply. A person who generates amazing PowerPoint presentations may be judged equally as competent in project management or budgeting, even though there is no reasonable evidence to support he or she has those skills.

Optimism Bias

The abilities to evaluate critically and to anticipate correctly are essential to risk-assessment and decision-making. When it comes to predicting how things will turn out once a decision is made, the optimism bias skews perspective and leads to overestimating the likelihood of a positive outcome and underestimating the likelihood of a negative outcome. People don't get married anticipating divorce, even though more than half of marriages end in divorce. It is common to overestimate our chances of winning the lottery, even though being crushed by a meteorite is more likely than scoring the jackpot.

This phenomenon is known as the optimism bias, and it is one of the most prevalent and robust biases documented in psychology and behavioral economics. It is especially dangerous in group decision-making, because a group of individuals with a natural tendency to be optimistic about an outcome will be even more optimistic as a group. Such optimism generates an illusion of control with a blindness to any evidence that points to a different outcome.

For example, suppose a team is tasked with determining the go-to-market strategy for a new product and they agree on a plan. With optimism bias at work, they will overestimate how well the plan will work while ignoring potential pitfalls or overlooking alternative perspectives. No one on the team is even thinking about possible obstacles or poor decisions even though a costly or irreparable outcome can be the result. This bias underlies the entire phenomena of groupthink.

Groupthink

Groupthink is a psychological phenomenon that occurs when people with a desire for harmony or conformity in the group make a group decision resulting in an irrational or unintended outcome. Social psychologist Irving Janis discovered this phenomenon in 1972, and it has become a debated topic in company culture regarding group decision-making.

Groupthink is characterized by a group of people so committed to reaching consensus that they put harmony and cohesion above diverse points of view and critical evaluation. For the "good of the group," members set aside their own thoughts, refrain from raising questions, or avoid exposing potential pitfalls. It's much easier to just agree with the group than be the one who is responsible for holding up progress even if it means generating a better idea or preventing the team from making a terrible plan.

Ironically, rather than producing a benefit for the group or organization, this approach often produces an "illusion of invulnerability" or an inflated and unrealistic certainty of the right decision. Groupthink can transform a harmonious team of bright, creative, independent thinkers into individuals stifling their best ideas and failing to identify the flaws in a given plan.

"Diversity is the art of thinking independently together."
-Malcolm Forbes

Overcoming the Influence of Bias

Biases can be hard at work undermining the efforts of even the most well-intended people without their knowledge. Only when we understand and acknowledge biases, as well as how they collectively impact the entire team, can an organization create an inclusive culture, maximize innovation and creativity, foster effective collabo-ration and communication, and engage and retain the best employees.

In team-based tasks or discussions, there are a few simple rules to put in place so that the best ideas aren't automatically dismissed, leading to poor decisions. Here are a few simple strategies that can help a team prevent bias from derailing organizational success.

1. Two-Minute Think Tank
Start or end a meeting by giving everyone two minutes to share a position on the given topic as well as key points to support that position. Use a timer to communicate that everyone has the same amount of "airtime," with clear expectations that all are to participate.

2. Leaders Speak Last
Great leaders know that they don't always have the best ideas, but some of the best employees will squash their own great ideas to support their leader. Establishing the rule that leaders speak last communicates that the leader doesn't have all the answers and is open and receptive to diverse perspectives.

3. The Worst First
Start the brainstorming session by generating a list of the worst ideas supported by reasons why they are the worst. Ask each team member to identify the worst possible idea, that is the worst idea that may, at first glance, seem like a plausible solution. These are the ideas that any number of constituents may shoot down for a number of reasons (i.e., cost-prohibitive, brand- misalignment, unsustainable, etc.)

This approach is not for a "thin-skinned" team, but it is a great way to counter the group-optimism effect and identify potential obstacles before they derail a project or cost a lot of money to fix down the road.

4. Divide and Conquer

Chunk the topic at hand into four or five subtopics and assign each to a small group or individual, allowing each person to be accountable for one piece of the project. This delegating approach gives everyone a sense of responsibility to the team and also communicates the notion that we are all experts of something, but none is an expert in everything.

5. Glass Half-Empty

Once a decision is reached, ask every member of the group to share an opposing opinion to test the strength of the position, forcing people to look past optimistic groupthink and poke holes in the decision. The purpose is not to persuade the group to adopt a different position but rather to confirm that the decision is sound, substantiated, and supported with data. Another approach is to conduct a pre-mortem as if the team had failed. In brainstorming all of the reasons for the failure, those involved may discover details or flaws not previously identified.

6. Celebrate Error Detectors

Reward those who find flaws that result in a change of course. When people realize that finding the flaws is essential to the process, critical thinking is encouraged, increasing the likelihood of making sound, well-founded decisions. Identifying flaws is not a natural tendency, especially in highly collaborative groups; however, invaluable time, money, and efforts are saved on the backend, reinforcing collective buy-in and accountability.

Often, the best learning is learning just how much we do not know and filling those gaps of knowledge with the expertise available. Ignorance may be bliss but only to the ignorant. Such bliss is costly as well as dangerous to those who recognize how much they do not know.

"Knowing what you don't know is much more useful than being brilliant."
-Charlie Munger

"Strive not to be a man of success, but rather to be one of value."

Life, Liberty, and the Pursuit of Happiness

Since the conception of this country, the pursuit of happiness has been woven into the very fabric of our national identity. "We hold these truths to be self-evident, that all men are created equal, that they are endowed by their Creator with certain unalienable Rights, that among these are Life, Liberty and the pursuit of Happiness."

There is no question as to what Thomas Jefferson meant by life and liberty. The Bill of Rights defines the right to life in the prohibition of cruel and unusual punishment and unlawful imprisonment, and the right to liberty as freedoms of religion, speech, and assembly. There is still some debate as to the meaning of happiness. Strangely, the word was not specifically defined as life and liberty were in the Bill of Rights, and it isn't guaranteed anywhere else in the Constitution. Is it possible that the founding fathers didn't define it because they couldn't agree on a definition? While historians speculate that back in 1776 happiness meant prosperity and financial security, it's not out of the realm of possibility that the framers agreed to disagree and left it up to us to decide.

Throughout history, thought leaders and philosophers have debated the meaning of happiness. Aristotle defined happiness in terms of hedonia (pleasure) and eudaimonia (a virtuous life). Plato asserted in *The Republic* that only those who are moral are happy. Thomas Aquinas maintained that while we can understand happiness through intellectual and moral virtues, the most perfect union with God is the most perfect human happiness and the goal of the whole of the human life. Viktor Frankl, Austrian neurologist, psychiatrist and Holocaust survivor, said that "happiness is dependent upon one's meaning of life, the value of suffering, and the responsibility to something greater than self."

In contemporary psychology, happiness is referred to as simply pleasure and meaning. Positive psychologists have recently added the distinct component of living a "good life" of work, family, friends, and hobbies to the definition. Even the definition is difficult to express without using a synonym. According to the *Oxford Dictionary*, happiness is quite simply the "state of being happy."

Happily Successful or Successfully Happy?

As a society, we've come to believe that happiness is measured by success, and success is measured by "stuff and status." While there's nothing inherently wrong with wanting a high-ranking position at work, a nice car, a house in a prestigious neighborhood, the danger lies in the assumption that they are the measures of happiness and fulfillment.

Ask ten people the measure of success and you'll likely get ten different answers. Like happiness, the meaning of success is unique to the individual, and the measure of success tends to be "status and stuff." Think about your own metrics for success. Maybe you define success as hitting your numbers this quarter or getting a promotion. Perhaps you feel successful when you finish a community project, raise money for a good cause, or celebrate your child's acceptance into college.

Consultants define success by the success of their clients. Teachers define success by the achievement of their students. For some, success could be something as simple as an "atta-boy" from your boss. We all have a unique and personal construct of success. Success feels good. Success makes us happy, right?

If we measure happiness by success, we'll never get there. Think of it like the mechanical rabbit at the racetrack. The dog never catches it. It's always just out of reach. Success works the same way. Each time we experience success, the definition changes. While getting the VP promotion may be the definition of success today, tomorrow success is becoming the CEO. To a parent who celebrates the success of a child's high school graduation, college graduation or career is the next metric. Each time we achieve a goal, the goal post for success moves and success means something different.

The go-to guy on happiness research is psychologist Daniel Kahneman, author of *Thinking Fast and Slow.* Much of

Kahneman's research explores cognitive traps that confuse our ability to differentiate being happy in life and being happy with life. One of those traps is the human phenomenon of "focusing illusion," our natural tendency to place undue importance on factors in the here and now while ignoring those factors that actually impact future happiness. Put more simply, it means "nothing in life is as important as you think it is, while you are thinking about it."

Kahneman maintains that happiness refers to two very different and contradictory viewpoints: one's present emotional state and one's overall satisfaction with life. How one feels today or this week is not a reliable indicator of one's overall satisfaction with life. A classic example of this construct is lottery winners. Many people think that the best thing that could ever happen to them is winning the lottery. Though there are stories of people whose lives improved after winning a big jackpot, there are more winners whose lives became worse.

Take, for example, Jack Whittaker. Jack won $315 million in 2002, the largest jackpot ever won by a single winning ticket in the history of American lottery. Before the win, he was the president of a successful contracting firm in West Virginia with a net worth of over $17 million. One morning, he stopped at a supermarket for a breakfast sandwich and bought $100 in tickets. Whittaker won and chose the cash option paying out $113,386,407 after taxes. Initially, Whittaker was quite generous and philanthropic. He pledged 10% of the winnings to Christian charities. He allocated $14 million to fund the Jack Whittaker Foundation, a nonprofit dedicated to helping low-income families in rural West Virginia. He bought the deli manager who sold him the breakfast sandwich and the tickets a house and a new Jeep Grand Cherokee, and he gave her a check for $44,000.

Less than a year after his big win, things began to go south. A briefcase containing $545,000 was stolen from his car while it was parked outside a strip club. When asked why he would carry that much money around with him, Whittaker replied, "Because I can." A year later, his office and home were broken into, and he was arrested twice for drunk driving. His granddaughter died under suspicious circumstances, and by 2007, he was broke. Caesars Atlantic City Casino sued him for bouncing $1.5 million worth of checks to cover gambling losses. In the end, Whittaker told reporters, "I wish I'd torn that ticket up."

Winning millions once and losing it is bad enough, but a second chance would give one the experience for redemption. Right? It would be logical think so, but Evelyn Basehore proved otherwise. Basehore won a $3.9 million jackpot in 1985. Five months later, she won the same game, winning another $1.4 million. She gave some money to friends and family, but most of the money went to the slot machines in Atlantic City. By 2000, she had lost all of it and moved into a trailer park in Brick, N.J.

In an effort to scientifically quantify that "money doesn't buy happiness," the most-well-known study was published in 1978 in the *Journal of Personality and Social Psychology*. Researchers measured and compared levels of happiness by conducting interviews with lottery winners, non-winners, and people who had suffered a terrible accident that left them paraplegic or quadriplegic.

They found that the overall happiness of lottery winners initially spiked, but after just a few months it returned to the same level as before they won. In terms of overall happiness, the lottery winners were not significantly happier than the non-winners. The accident victims were slightly less happy, but not by much. The study showed that most people have a set level of happiness and that even after life-changing events either positive or negative, people tend to return to that set point.

People generally think they will be happier with a big positive event like a lottery win or a promotion and a raise. Effects diminish over time when the novelty of the new conditions wears off. In addition, that big win doesn't change the other things that impact happiness like parents, siblings, mindset, or basic disposition.

Perhaps the most significant implication of this research is just how bad we are at predicting what will make us happy in the future. Psychologists call this *affective forecasting*, and it's particularly true when it comes to money. For example, research shows that the majority of employees report feeling greater happiness when they are have flexible work schedules, greater autonomy in their roles, or expressed appreciation from the boss over an increase in salary. Yet, when asked they are specifically asked what would make them happy, "more money" is the answer more times than not.

"The part of our brain that enables us to think about the future is one of nature's newest inventions, so it isn't surprising that when we try to use this new ability to imagine our futures, we make some rookie errors."
-Dan Gilbert

Another cognitive trap Kahneman identifies is our confusion between experiences and memories of experiences. He explains that we have two selves: an experiencing self, who lives in the present, and the remembering self, who is the story teller. What we get to keep from our experiences are the stories our remembering self tells. The remembering self is also the decision maker. We make decisions based upon memories of experiences, not the experiences. He claims that because experience and memory are fundamentally different, happiness means something different to the remembering self and the experiencing self. Happiness of the experiencing self is measured by the happiness we feel in the moment. Happiness of the remembering self is measured by how happy we feel when we think about our life as a whole. The distinction lies in the gap between how we *think about our lives* and how we *live our lives*.

Kahneman found that most people naturally go to greater lengths to protect themselves from a bad experience than they do to experience something good. This choice is made because the brain tends to respond more intensely to negative things than to equally intense positive things. Memories define experiences more than experiences define memories.

"We don't choose between experiences; we choose between memories of experiences. We think of our future as anticipated memories."
-Daniel Kahneman

Imagine you just returned from a 10-day cruise in the Mediterranean. The weather was great, the excursions were fantastic, and the Italian delicacies were delicious. One bad mussel didn't agree with you, however, and you spent the rest of that day in bed. While the other nine days of the vacation may have been magical, that single negative experience is likely to create a much more powerful memory. Years later, you may only vaguely remember the picturesque drive along the Amalfi Coast or the homemade Limoncello in Sorrento, but the day you were puking up dry toast in your cabin will seem like yesterday. The entire trip may be tainted by this single negative event. Such a reaction is all part of the negativity bias in our implicit memory that shapes the way we perceive experiences.

Happiness in the Workplace

The pursuit of happiness has taken on global significance since 2012. In July 2011, the UN General Assembly initiated *The World Happiness Report* to define and measure happiness in countries around the world in order to guide public policy. The first report was released on April 1, 2012. Since then, each year experts in fields of economics, psychology, and national statistics assess the progress of nations into issues relating to happiness, ethics, and policy implications. *The World Happiness Report* released on

March 14, 2018, ranked 156 countries by their happiness levels, and 117 countries by the happiness of their immigrants. Finland ranked the happiest country in the world with Norway, Denmark, and Iceland following at the top. Each year, countries shift up or down a bit depending upon the focus, but one thing doesn't change much: The happiest countries are among the wealthiest in the world.

Ahhh... so money does buy happiness! Not so fast. *The Gallup World Poll*, which has been surveying people in over 150 countries around the world since 2006, analyzes data and investigates the extent to which people experience positive and negative affective states like enjoyment, stress, and worry in their day-to-day lives, as well as more workplace-specific measures such as job satisfaction and employee engagement.

According to the *2017 Gallup State of American Workforce Report*, higher income does correlate with higher feelings of happiness but only to a certain point. A study conducted at Princeton confirmed that the lower a person's annual income falls below $75,000, the unhappier he or she feels. But no matter how much more than $75,000 people make, they don't report any greater degree of happiness. The top two factors of job satisfaction were (1) *the ability to do what I do best,* and (2) *greater work-life balance and personal well-being.*

There is an irrefutable correlation between personal happiness and professional success. People do not want to compromise one at the expense of the other. There are numerous studies that show how one's happiness in life is influenced by happiness in the workplace and vice versa. A 2017 study conducted at Oregon University explored the impact of a healthy sex life on job satisfaction and engagement. Researchers found that married employees who prioritized sex at home enjoyed an advantage at work the next day with greater productivity, engagement, and enjoyment in their work tasks.

Other studies show that even short-term boosts in happiness at home can lead to greater productivity at work. This job satisfaction and productivity leads to a higher level of employee loyalty. Ultimately, happy employees and a positive work environment translate to greater employee productivity, loyalty, and engagement, a better definition of success for the employees and the company.

Scandinavian countries have consistently ranked high as the world's happiest countries. They have also applied the "happiness research" to create happy workplaces. They even have a word for it: *arbejdsglæde* means "work happiness." They believe that people who are happy at work have better health, are more successful and enjoy higher incomes, and are happier with their lives. To them, being happy at work is not a luxury; it's a necessity for a good life.

Do What You Love? Or Love What You Do?

Confucius said, "Choose a job you love, and you will never have to work a day in your life." Since then, the most prolific thought leaders have contributed wise words about seeking a career that fills one with passion or aligns with purpose. Yet, current statistics showing how many people are disengaged and dissatisfied at work are indicators that most people are not heeding the wise man's advice.

Given that we spend so much of our time and energy at work, is it possible to be unhappy at work and still enjoy a happy life? Perhaps Steve Jobs was on to something when he flipped that advice upside down to "love what you do."

"Sometimes life hits you in the head with a brick. Don't lose faith. I'm convinced that the only thing that kept me going was that I loved what I did. You've got to find what you love. And that is as true for your work as it is for your lovers. Your work is going to fill a large part of your life, and the only way to be truly satisfied is to do what you believe is great work. And the only way to do great work is to love what you do. If you haven't found it yet, keep looking. Don't settle. As with all matters of the heart, you'll know when you find it. And, like any great relationship, it just gets better and better as the years roll on. So, keep looking until you find it. Don't settle."

- Steve Jobs, Stanford, 2005.

We live in a society that works long and hard. Most of us spend between 40-60 hours each week at work. On average, that is about one third of one's lifespan. Ask ten people how they feel about their lives at work, and statistically speaking only three will say that they have fulfilling jobs that are engaging, challenging, personally rewarding, and aligned with their talents and skills. A recent poll shows that more than 70% of Americans are "unhappy, uninspired, and disengaged" at work.

How many of them go home to their families with a happy, inspired, and engaged mindset? Is it even possible to "balance" that kind of negativity in a meaningful way? And for remote workers, stepping away from the office may seem impossible. As technology makes connecting with colleagues as far away as your nearest device, finding a balance between work and life becomes increasingly challenging.

The reality is that work is not separate from life; it is a part of life. It can be meaningful and rewarding or distracting and disruptive. But trying to compartmentalize work from life and balance them as contrasting forces is an exercise in futility. The human brain just doesn't work that way. We don't use separate areas of the brain at work than what we use at home, and the stress we feel at work isn't confined to the workplace and doesn't magically disappear when we leave. Stress in one area of life spills over into other areas of life. Likewise, happiness in one area of life spills over into other areas of life.

Apply that concept to the workplace: Happy employees contribute to organizational happiness, and organizational happiness significantly contributes to organizational success. When people are happy, engaged, and contributing, the team is successful. When the team is successful, the members are happier, more engaged, and more willing to contribute. From an organizational standpoint, that's the money shot. When we flip that around and correlate individual happiness with individual success, the construct changes.

The harder I work, the more successful I'll be.
The more successful I am, the happier I'll be.

It's easy to get sucked into this logic. The problem is that it's scientifically twisted. There are more than three decades of research that explain what happens in the brain when we experience happiness. Not only do we feel better when we're happy, our brain chemistry physically changes. When we are positive, the brain becomes more engaged, creative, and productive, and that brain activity increases motivation, creative thought, energy, and resilience.

Remember all of those happy chemicals? Dopamine, serotonin, oxytocin, and endorphins are released when we experience positive emotions, and they activate the prefrontal cortex in the upstairs brain. When these chemicals are flowing, the thinking, rational part of the brain is in charge. When we are stressed, fearful, angry, or threatened, the stress chemicals are released to signal the downstairs brain to prepare for fight or flight, and the thinking, rational brain is paused to allocate all of the resources to manage the threat. The brain is literally hardwired to perform best when we are happy. A more accurate construct would be:

The happier I am, the better my brain works.
The better my brain works, the more successful I'll be.

Psychology expert and author of *"The Happiness Advantage"* Shawn Achor maintains that happiness is not the belief that we don't need to change; it is the realization that we can. When we shift our thinking and understand that happiness is not a mood but rather a work ethic and a choice, every single business and educational opportunity improves. This discovery has been borne out repeatedly by rigorous research in psychology and neuroscience, management studies, and the bottom lines of organizations around the world. His research shows a direct correlation between a positive mindset and professional success. Among his findings: Sales of happy people are 37% higher, productivity is 31% better, and they are 40% more likely to receive a promotion.

If we know that happiness determines success, why aren't people just happier? Psychologists like Sonja Lyubomirsky at the Greater Good Science Center have been exploring that question to find out just how much control we have over being happy. Lyubomirsky maintains that one's level of happiness is contingent upon three primary factors: genetic predisposition, external events, and intentional activities.

According to Lyubomirsky, only 10% of our happiness is defined by things we have no control over (losing a job, a car accident, a death in the family), and 50% is attributed to our genetic predisposition for happiness. The remaining 40% is defined by what she calls intentional activity or our behaviors, thoughts, and attitudes. Even the 50% genetic baseline is just a predisposition to happiness, meaning that you can rewire your brain to change it. And that intentional activity which defines 40% of our happiness is entirely within our control.

That 40% of intentional activity is largely shaped by three factors:
1. optimism (control over things that matter)
2. social connectedness (positive interactions with others)
3. perception of stress (challenges, fear, anxieties, or threats)

Think about how you feel when you see negative news stories in the media, events over which you have no control such as terrorist attacks, murders, and other crimes, or a plummeting stock market. If you don't think seeing these stories impacts your personal happiness and productivity, think again.

Dr. Seligman studied the long-term impact of negative and positive news stories on the public, this time with *The Huffington Post*. Participants were randomly placed into two groups, and each group was shown televised news stories. One group watched three minutes of negative news stories. The second group watched three minutes of solution-focused news stories of resilience, courage, and accomplishment. It's important to note that these weren't just fun stories of giggling babies or cats watching birds. These were gritty stories about people who persevered and triumphed. For example, one story reported on inner-city kids working hard to win a school competition. Another highlighted a 70-year-old man who finally passed his GED after failing numerous times.

Six hours later, participants were asked to complete a survey that included questions to measure their mood and stress level. The people who watched just three minutes of negative news in the morning were 27% more likely to report having a bad day six to eight hours later. Conversely, people who watched the same number of solution-focused stories were 88% more likely to report having a good day six to eight hours later. Positivity and negativity both have sticking power.

Remember the bad chemicals? Visualize what happens to the person who sees the negative worldview. His brain is so busy producing all of the stress-fighting chemicals, there is very little bandwidth left to think, process information, be creative, or even recognize the positive events that produce dopamine, oxytocin, and serotonin.

The longer one remains in that vicious cycle, the harder it is to get out of it because of the over-production of cortisol. Eventually, it snowballs to the point where anything good seems completely out of reach and the "why bother?"

attitude takes over. Psychologists call this *learned helplessness*, and there is a direct correlation between learned helplessness, chronic failure, and depression. We'll dig deeper into this in the next chapter.

Happiness isn't just being content with the life we have. It's the optimistic belief that we have control over making our lives better.

"There are only two ways to live life. One is as though nothing is a miracle and the other is as though everything is a miracle."

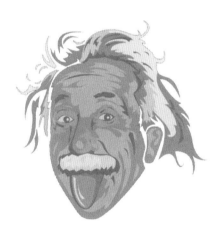

The Attitude of Gratitude

"You may never have proof of your importance, but you are more important than you think. There are always those who couldn't do without you. The rub is that you don't always know who."

That little nugget is from Robert Fulghum's book, *All I Really Need to Know I Learned in Kindergarten*. By the time we can tie our shoes, we know the importance of saying "thank you." It's one of the first social courtesies we're taught. Somewhere between the kindergarten classroom and the rat race of life, the practice of gratitude can be lost.

Expressing gratitude is not just good manners. Of all the areas studied in the field of positive psychology, gratitude has perhaps the most extensive body of research. Studies show that gratitude is a potent agent in the construction of our mental models. It changes the lens through which we view the world and forces us to acknowledge the good things, both big and small, that are so easy to take for granted. *I have a job. The sun is shining. It felt good to laugh with a friend. I'm alive.*

Grateful people have been shown to have higher levels of positive effect, a greater sense of belonging, and lower levels of depression and stress. A wealth of research substantiates the positive physical and emotional benefits of gratitude.

Researchers at the National Institutes of Health examined the neural activity and blood flow in various regions of the brain while people experienced gratitude. They found that higher levels of gratitude generated increased activity in the hypothalamus which is responsible for some pretty essential body functions such as eating, drinking, sleeping, metabolic activity, and managing stress levels.

In addition, feelings of gratitude directly activate the limbic system and trigger a release of dopamine. Dopamine is the reward chemical, but it is also responsible for initiating the action to get that good feeling again. It's the brain saying, "Oh... that felt good! Do that again!"

That shot of dopamine is also what launches the brain into what neuroscientists call the virtuous cycle. As complex as the human brain is, it has a one-track mind, preferring to focus on either positive stimuli or negative stimuli but not both at the same time. When the brain is focused on positive events, the natural tendency is to stay in that positive loop until a negative experience ultimately intervenes and breaks the cycle.

Conversely, the brain can also get stuck in a negative loop called a vicious cycle, what I like to call the WMS or "Why

Me Syndrome." When the brain becomes trapped in the vicious cycle, negatives become the focus. *The traffic made me late for work, someone took my parking place, I spilled my coffee, it's raining and I forgot my umbrella, my boss is a jerk.* There may be many positive things going on, but the brain is too busy with the negatives to notice them.

The brain also has a natural tendency to look for things that prove what it believes to be true. Remember confirmation bias? It can be a driving force behind one's focus. For example, one who begins the day with the expectation that it will be miserable primes the brain to search for evidence to make that happen. Conversely, starting the day with the belief that life is good will prime the brain to search for evidence to confirm that worldview. The outlook we choose determines whether we get stuck in the virtuous cycle or the vicious cycle. What we find depends mainly upon what we look for.

> *If you focus on what you have in life,*
> *you'll always have more than enough.*
> *If you focus on what you don't have in life,*
> *you'll never have enough.*
> *-Oprah Winfrey*

A gratitude study conducted by researcher and author Robert Emmons explored how gratitude impacts both physical health and outlook on life. Participants were randomly assigned to one of three groups. All three groups were given a weekly journaling assignment for a total of ten weeks.

One group was asked to record five things that happened during each week for which each was grateful. The second group was asked to record five obstacles or challenges they experienced each week. The third group was instructed to record five events from the week that had an impact on each but was not told whether to focus on positive or negative events.

The participants in the first group who recorded positive expressions of gratitude reported fewer physical aches and pains, less stress, and greater optimism about the upcoming week compared to the other two groups. These participants also exercised an average of 1.5 hours more and made more significant progress toward personal goals than those in the other groups.

Emmons expanded his research to explore the impact of gratitude on adults suffering from neuromuscular disease. After participants had completed a 21-day gratitude program, researchers sought to determine if there were any physical and socioemotional differences compared to a control group. The gratitude group demonstrated an increase in energy, positive moods, better quality and duration of sleep, as well as a greater sense of connectedness compared to the control group.

Gratitude: The Gateway to Optimism

Exploring gratitude in isolation of optimism is impossible. Scientists have been studying the reciprocal benefits of gratitude and optimism to determine how they influence everything from cognition and productivity to happiness and overall health. Recent research indicates that optimists and pessimists approach problems differently, and these differences result in a variety of ways of coping with adversity.

We often have no control over the inevitable hurdles, hardships, and heartbreaks of life, but we can control our reactions and our mental perspective. People who practice gratitude have a more positive outlook on life and are better able to navigate through the tough times, feeling empowered rather than victimized. Numerous studies show that it is this appreciation and positivity that enables us to see opportunities and to develop resilience.

The mere act of positive thinking can boost a person's immune system, protect against harmful behaviors, prevent stress-related disease, and even predict longevity. Among psychological constructs, optimism and gratitude may be two of the most important predictors of overall physical and emotional well-being. Quite simply, gratitude and optimism make us smarter, healthier, and happier.

How full or how empty you see the glass depends upon how grateful you are for the glass.

Learned Optimism and Learned Helplessness

For many years, we believed that one's disposition, either optimistic or pessimistic, was hardwired into personality. New research, however, indicates otherwise. Dr. Martin Seligman, the father of positive psychology, has explored the concepts of learned optimism and learned helplessness for more than 25 years. His studies show that we can teach ourselves to see opportunities and solutions or we can teach ourselves to be helpless.

Learned helplessness is a phenomenon observed in both humans and animals that have been exposed to adverse stimuli such as pain or discomfort. He found that humans, dogs, rats, mice, and even cockroaches that experienced mildly painful electric shocks over which they had no control would eventually just accept the treatment. They had learned to be helpless even when they were given a way to avoid the shock.

Strangely, however, he found that about a third of the subjects who experience the adverse stimuli never become helpless. What is it about them? Seligman says the answer is optimism.

To illustrate, imagine an optimist and a pessimist each applies for that "dream job." Both are invited back for the second round of interviews and asked to give a short presentation. They both believe that they made great impressions though neither of them was offered the job. The optimist thinks, "Wow... I really thought I nailed that interview. The guy who got the job must have had an amazing presentation. Maybe mine could have been better." The pessimist thinks, "I knew I wouldn't get hired! I'll never get my dream job. I'm such a failure!"

This scenario is an excellent example of two opposite *explanatory styles*. Seligman describes explanatory styles as the stories we tell ourselves to explain why things happen the way they do. He maintains that optimists and pessimists are easy to identify based upon three fundamental attributions, the "3Ps."

Personal: the degree to which the event happened because of internal factors or external factors
I wonder if I could have done something differently to change the outcome, or *nothing I could do would have changed things.*

Permanent: the degree to which the event is permanent or temporary
I'll never be good at this, or *I can get better at this.*

Pervasive: the extent to which the event is perceived as global or specific
I'm a complete failure, or *this just isn't one of my strengths.*

The pessimist views his inability to land the job as internal, unchangeable, and pervasive, whereas the optimist is already thinking about the next opportunity. The way we explain life's events to ourselves determines whether we bounce back from rejection, disappointment, and defeat, or simply give up. Seligman's theory is that this difference in attitude enables optimists to be happier, more resilient, and more successful than pessimists. In his book, *Learned Optimism: How to Change Your Mind and Your Life*, he writes,

"The optimists and the pessimists: I have been studying them for the past twenty-five years. The defining characteristic of pessimists is that they tend to believe bad events will last a long time, will undermine everything they do, and are completely their fault. The optimists, who are confronted with the same hard knocks of this world, think about misfortune oppositely. They tend to believe defeat is just a temporary setback, that its causes are confined to this one case. The optimists believe defeat is not their fault. Circumstances, bad luck, or other people may be responsible. Such people are unfazed by defeat. Confronted by a bad situation, they perceive it as a challenge and try harder."

Much of Seligman's research explores the impact of optimism and gratitude on stress, depression, anxiety, and even as indicators of professional success. The detrimental effects of stress on the brain and body are well-documented. Scientists have linked increased levels of stress to a host of ailments, everything from headaches to immune-system disorders to cardiovascular disease. While none of us is immune to stress, optimists manage it better and revert to a state of calm quickly after a stressful event. Learned optimism techniques have also been shown to decrease anxiety issues and depression with correlating physical benefits.

Increased optimism has also been linked to professional success. Studies have shown that optimism and positivity significantly impact how people are perceived in the workplace. Optimistic people smile and laugh more, making them appear more confident, trustworthy, and collaborative. They also demonstrate greater motivation and energy to be productive. For all of these reasons, optimists are more likely to enjoy promotions and salary increases than their pessimistic peers.

Seligman tested his optimism theory in a real-world case study with Metropolitan Life. In the mid-1980s, Metropolitan Life was hiring an average of 5,000 salespeople each year and spending more than $30K each to train them over the course of two years. Of all the new hires, half quit the first year and four out of five within four years. Do the math: the return on investment was terrible. MetLife wanted to identify people who would be more resilient in the training process, better problem-solvers, and ultimately more successful salespeople, and they hired Dr. Seligman to find them.

Seligman tracked 15,000 new MetLife consultants who had taken two tests. One test was the company's standard screening exam and the other was Seligman's profile designed to measure optimism. He was able to identify one segment of the new hires that failed the company test but scored as "super-optimists" on his profile test. Despite failing the company test, this group outsold the pessimists who passed the company test by 21% in the first year and 57% in the second.

In 1995, Seligman extended this study to examine the impact of optimism in other industries, including insurance, office products, real estate, banking, and car sales. The results across all studies indicated that optimists outsold pessimists by 20 to 40%.

In another landmark study, Seligman explored the neuroscience of gratitude as a potential treatment for mental illness. He wanted to find out which types of gratitude practices would not only make people happier, but which could combat depression with the most long-lasting effects. He divided 577 participants into four different groups. Each group was given a specific task to complete in one week. They were then tested immediately after the task and then again one week, one month, three months, and six months after the task to determine how long the effects of that weeklong exercise would last.

Control group:
Participants were asked to write about their early memories every night for one week.

Gratitude visit group:
Participants were given one week to write and then deliver in person a letter of gratitude to someone who had been exceptionally kind to them but had never been properly thanked.

Three good things group:
Participants were asked to write down three good things about each day for one week. They were also told to write down what they thought caused those positive things to happen.

You at your best group:
Participants were asked to write about a time when they were at their best and then to reflect on the personal strengths that this experience exemplified. They were also told to reflect upon those experiences by reading the journal entry once each day for a week.

It may not be a surprise to learn that Seligman found an increase in happiness and a decrease in depression after all of these reflection exercises. The most significant difference between the groups, though, was the length of time that the positive changes lasted.

Participants in the control group and the "you at your best" group showed a boost in happiness and a reduction in depression immediately following the exercise. The effects significantly diminished after one month, however, and were no longer apparent after three months.

Participants in the "gratitude visit" group showed the most significant positive changes in the entire study. The boost in happiness and the decrease in depressive symptoms were maintained at follow-up assessments one week and one month later, though the effects began to diminish after the one-month mark.

The biggest surprise was the "three good things" group, which demonstrated the most long-lasting gains. Beneficial effects appeared one month following the post test. At the one-month follow-up, participants in this exercise were happier and less depressed than they had been at baseline, and they continued to demonstrate the positive effects at the three-month and six-month assessments.

Optimism and Gratitude on Relationships

All of these gains' positive outlook, physical energy, mental health, motivation toward goals' also have a direct impact on the quality of relationships. Dr. John Gottman at the University of Washington wanted to determine if there were quantifiable patterns of behavior that would accurately predict the longevity of marriage. Over the past 20 years, he has conducted numerous longitudinal studies and developed a methodology to rate how couples interacted, how positive or negative their expressions were, and how those expressions translated to the spouses.

Gottman maintains that he can predict with 90% accuracy which marriages will make it and which will end in divorce by observing and calculating the positive and negative expressions when they interact. Unless the couple can maintain a ratio of 5:1 positive to negative, the marriage is more likely to fail. His formula weights negative expressions and positive expressions differently. According to Gottman, it takes five positive expressions of gratitude, appreciation, or love to counter one negative expression of anger, frustration, or disappointment.

The exact causal effects between optimism, gratitude, and good emotional and physical health are still a topic of debate. Some researchers theorize that optimists are more health-conscious because they believe in the potential positive outcomes. Others maintain that people who are more positive and express appreciation for the people around them are healthier because they are more likeable and therefore have stronger social networks and relationships. Still others attribute health benefits to the inverse correlation with stress.

There is no question that grateful people who see the glass as half full enjoy what's in the glass far more than their pessimistic counterparts. All of us are capable of nurturing optimism. So, on those gloomy days when your happiness meter isn't registering, the best way to change that outlook may be to express gratitude to someone else.

Walk down the hall to thank a colleague for being on the team. Pick up the phone for the sole purpose of saying, "You're special to me." Grab a notepad and write a heartfelt expression of thanks. To make that happiness last, incorporate it as part of your routine by looking for three good things every day.

That old saying, "What we find depends upon what we look for" is so true! Begin each day with the intention of looking for three good things, and most likely more than three will appear. On the really tough days, those good things are going to mean even more.

Gratitude Gains in the Workplace

When was the last time you were recognized at work? When was the last time you expressed gratitude to another coworker? Do you remember how you felt? I will bet that you do. While the personal benefits of gratitude seem apparent, there are professional gains as well.

Integrating gratitude into an organization doesn't need to be an HR initiative rolled out from the leadership team. Whether it's a simple "thank you" note or a more formal expression of appreciation, the psychological effects of gratitude in the workplace can have a tremendous impact on job satisfaction, effort, productivity, and corporate culture. Every one of us has the power to put gratitude to work, from the custodian to the CEO.

Just as in our personal lives, a sense of gratitude can improve self-esteem, optimism, a sense of unity, and overall well-being at work. Remember the concept of emotional contagion? When we extend expressions of gratitude among our colleagues, we create a "pay-it-forward" chain of positivity that makes the entire organization more successful. As additional people feel the effects, the number people paying it forward increases. The dopamine effect is a powerful force. If you don't think one person is powerful enough to be a catalyst for positive organizational change, think again.

Tracy Gallimore is the Vice President of Xenial. As a leader in the quick-service and fast-casual markets, the organization has enjoyed steady growth. One of the challenges that often accompanies growth is maintaining a healthy corporate culture. After working with Tracy and his leadership team in a professional-development session, I asked each of them to identify one or two nuggets they could put into practice immediately.

The guiding mantra of the organization is that "everything we do matters," and Tracy recognizes that philosophy only works if *everyone matters*. The concept of gratitude really resonated with him. It wouldn't take a lot of time, and for a guy who was very much about making lists and checking boxes, Tracy felt this approach would be an excellent way to stay focused on the people.

Recently, Tracy shared his experience of writing and delivering that first thank you note. He sketched out a genuine message of appreciation on a little piece of paper and left it for an employee to find on his keyboard when he arrived the next morning. "I felt like Santa Claus!" Tracy told me. "It was just a quick hand-drawn note, but it felt so good to think about him finding it the next morning." The reaction from the recipient was much different than that from the casual, "Hey, good job!" that we so often give or receive. The employee was grateful, genuinely grateful, for Tracy's simple yet genuine expression of appreciation.

Perhaps what surprised Tracy most was what has happened after he wrote that first note. First, he was amazed at how contagious something as simple as an expression of gratitude can be. The organization already had a formal employee recognition program in place, and nurturing a healthy culture was already an established priority. Tracy noticed people at all levels of the organization reinforcing those values by informally recognizing one another for contributions, victories, and even challenges.

Tracy could have called a meeting with HR and directed them to incorporate the "weekly-thank-you-note" component into the existing program. Instead, the altruistic, organic nature of this new mindset not only reinforced that program from the bottom up, but it was a meaningful way for individuals at every level of the organization to take ownership of that culture. It wasn't an initiative; it wasn't a mandate. It wasn't a responsibility defined by a committee or a position. It became an individual choice to recognize people who matter, and it was contagious!

The second big surprise for Tracy was how being in the market of gratitude, looking for those things for which to be grateful, changed his perspective. "It's easy to focus on the problems and the obstacles," he told me, "but, when I know I'm going to write a note that day and I'm looking for the good things, I see so many positive things I may have otherwise missed."

Dopamine and good vibrations aside, does the gratitude-factor actually impact the bottom line of the organization? Francesca Gino at Harvard Business School and Adam Grant of the Wharton School of Business at the University of Pennsylvania say these ingredients do matter. They explored how being thanked and the perception of being valued affected competence and productivity.

In their first experiment, participants were asked to provide feedback on a fictitious cover letter. Half of the subjects received confirmation of their feedback while the other half received a message that expressed gratitude for completing the task. When the researchers measured the subjects' sense of self-worth afterward, 25% of the group that received confirmation felt higher self-worth compared to 55% of the group that received thanks.

The second experiment was an extension of that same group of subjects. Each was asked to provide feedback on another fictitious cover letter. More than double the number of students in the gratitude group (66%) agreed to provide feedback on the second letter compared to only 32% in the group who received no gratitude.

The "gratitude effect" was explored again in a field study to determine how it impacted productivity. The subjects were fundraisers who all received a fixed salary regardless of the number of calls they made. The director visited one group in person to express his appreciation for the job that they did and the contributions they were making to the organization.

The second group did not receive a visit from the director or any expressions of gratitude for their work. That simple demonstration of gratitude generated an increase in the number of calls by more than 50% over the previous week while the calls of those who had not received thanks remained the same as the previous week.

Still not convinced? An employee survey of more than 2,000 adults conducted by Harris Interactive on behalf of Glassdoor revealed that gratitude is a significant driver in employee satisfaction and engagement. A vast majority (81%) of employees reported that they're motivated to work harder when their boss shows appreciation for their work compared to only 37% motivated by the fear of losing their job, and 38% motivated by a demanding boss. Moreover, more than half (53%) of the employees reported they would stay longer at their company if they felt more appreciation from their boss.

Making Gratitude a Habit

"We are what we repeatedly do.
Excellence, then, is not an act, but a habit."
-Aristotle

It's human nature to get complacent with the things that give us comfort, and it's very easy to take them for granted. Natural disasters like devastating floods, hurricanes and forest fires that claim lives, destroy entire communities, and cost billions to rebuild are good examples.

When we hear about these disasters, most of us empathize and sympathize with the plights of those involved. We may be grateful that everything we own isn't floating down the street. Maybe we feel compelled to reach out to help in some way. Still, how quickly we forget! That gratitude fades away and seems to have disappeared completely only a few days later with complaints about rain after just washing the car or grumbles about a ruined family picnic.

An old saying reminds, "If you've forgotten the language of gratitude, you'll never be on speaking terms with happiness." Beyond happiness, we now know that gratitude can be a powerful catalyst for personal and professional growth, mental and physical health, and an overall sense of well-being. To reap all of those benefits, though, it must become a habit, a behavior that is so second-nature that it feels odd not to do it. Simple, right?

Can you think of a time when you really wanted to create a healthy habit in your life? Maybe you wanted to cut out sweets, drink more water, or hit the gym regularly. We've all been there with the best of intentions driving us for a while and then gradually fading away; however, the difference between intention and habit is automaticity. This notion of acting without thinking is a central driver of habits. And it helps to answer the question: How long does it take to make gratitude a habit?

Some "experts" report that it takes 21 days to form a habit while others will argue it takes 30 days or 60 days. Perhaps the best answer is: *It depends on the habit and the person.* A research team led by Phillapa Lally at University College of London sought to answer that very question. Participants in the study were asked to choose a behavior they wanted to turn into a daily habit. They asked them to record whether or not they performed their habit each day and rate how automatic it felt to them.

As you might expect, the variance between participants to get to a repeated level of automaticity was wide and depended upon a variety of variables such as the complexity of the habit and the frequency and consistency of the practice. The average was 66 days, but some people needed over 250 days to make a specific behavior second nature, more than 25 weeks!

Most will admit that committing to anything for 25 weeks seems pretty daunting. It is really easy to get psyched out or lose focus when the goal seems unattainable or the finish line is too far away. But, what about 28 days? Could you commit to something for 28 days if there was just a chance that it could positively impact your life? That doesn't seem nearly so hard, does it?

500 Minutes ... 28 Days

If you could be happier and make your brain work better by doing one simple thing every day for 28 days, would you do it? What if I told you that you'd only have to spend about 15 minutes a day to make gratitude a life-changing, brain-changing habit?

The most important investment you can make for yourself is *in yourself*. There is no magic pill or secret sauce to increase happiness or success. There is, however, science. Use that science in your journey to a more grateful you, a more successful you, and a happier you. The companion journal to this book, *Happier Hour with Einstein: Gratitude Journal*, applies the principles of the neuroscience in this book to help cultivate the practice of gratitude as a daily habit.

Each full-color daily entry also incorporates the science of neuroaesthetics to help facilitate introspection and visualization. Founded in 2002, neuroaesthetics is defined as "the scientific study of aesthetic experiences at the neurological level." Put more simply, it's the convergence of neuroscience and empirical aesthetics, or what happens in the brain while creating or perceiving art. Scientists in this field strive to understand the neural processes underlying artistic experiences such as perception, interpretation, and emotion. A large part of the research has focused on the visual qualities that humans find universally appealing such as those related to color, form, or spatial arrangement and how those aesthetic preferences influence brain activity and emotional responses.

While this emerging field has been met with criticism from the broader scientific community, the concept of bridging brain science and the visual arts has grown over the last decade with increasing international interest. In a 2014 study published by Vered Aviv in Frontiers in Human Neuroscience, one very specific question was explored: What does abstract art do to the viewer's mind?

Aviv found that abstract art evoked responses in parts of the brain that are activated by all types of art such as landscapes, still life, and portraits. Because abstract images do not consist of clearly recognizable objects, they are processed through pathways less familiar and less utilized. More simply, the brain tends to process abstract images with the whole brain because they don't fit in one specific region. Free flowing shapes, colors, and lines, therefore, open the mind to think in a less restrictive manner enabling us to form new associations, activate more positive emotions, and potentially form new creative pathways.

We also know that color and mood are inextricably linked. We have innate reactions to colors, and they have psychological properties that relate to the body, mind, emotions and the essential balance between all three. For example, red is a stimulating color that increases your heart rate and grabs your attention. Blue is on the other end of the psychological spectrum as it decreases blood pressure. Softer blues calm the mind while stronger blues may stimulate clear thought.

The energy we feel from color is both dynamic and personal, and it varies depending on culture, personality, and even the circumstances of the moment. While the soft, free-flowing images on the journal pages are blended washes of colors, the psychological properties may help you harness deeper introspection as you think about each day.

The full-color pages include watercolor flowers, leaves, and other natural images. The positive effects of nature on mood, stress, and mental functioning are well-established. Studies show that regardless of age, gender, or culture, nature has a calming effect on most of us. Being in nature or simply viewing images of natural scenes or objects reduces anger, fear, anxiety, and stress and is shown to increase pleasant feelings and overall well-being.

Each spread in the journal has a morning entry for you to envision the day you want to live and identify the steps you need to take to make it happen and an evening entry for grateful reflection. Commit to 28 days of intentional focus, inspirational thoughts, and "daily dares" designed to keep you focused on the positive people in your life and grateful reflection. It will change the way you see yourself and the world around you.

Aren't you worth a few intentional minutes each day to be the very best version of yourself?

References

Achor, Shawn. *The Happiness Advantage: The Seven Principles That Fuel Success and Performance at Work,* 2011.

Aviv, Vered. What does the brain tell us about abstract art? *Frontiers in Human Neuroscience*, 28 February 2014.

Azab, Marwa. Is social pain real pain? *Psychology Today*. Published online 2017, April 25.

Berk, Lee and Tan, Stanley A. Cortisol and Catecholamine Stress Hormone Decrease Is Associated with the Behavior of Perceptual Anticipation of Mirthful Laughter. *The FASEB Journal.* 2008;22:946.11.

Brickman, Philip; Coates, Dan; Janoff-Bulman, Ronnie. Lottery winners and accident victims: Is happiness relative? *Journal of Personality and Social Psychology, 36*(8), 917-927.

Brown, Brené . *Rising Strong: How the Ability to Reset Transforms the Way We Live, Love, Parent and Lead.* Randon House Trade Paperbacks. 2017.

Brown, Sunni. The Doodle Revolution: Unlock the Power to Think Differently, 2015.

Bolkan, San; Andersen, Peter. Image induction and social influence: Explication and initial tests. *Basic and Applied Social Psychology.* 2009, Vol 31, Issue 4.

Centorrino, Samuele; Djemai, Elodie; Hopfensitz, Astrid; Milinski, Manfred; Seabright, Paul. Honest signaling in trust interactions: smiles rated as genuine induce trust and signal higher earning opportunities. *Evolution and Human Behavior.* January 2015, Volume 36, Issue 1.

Cranston, Susie; Keller, Scott. Increasing the 'meaning quotient' of work. *McKinsey Quarterly.* 2013, Jan.

Dell'Amore, Christine. Rejection really hurts, brain scans show. *National Geographic News.* Published online 2011, March 30.

Duckworth, Angela. *Grit: The Power of Passion and Perseverence.* Scribner Publishing, 2016.

Dweck, Carol. *Mindset: The New Psychology of Success.* Ballantyne Books, 2006.

Emmons, Robert. http://emmons.faculty.ucdavis.edu

Filkukova P. and Klempe, SH. Rhyme as reason in commercial and social advertising. *Scandinavian Journal of Psychology.* 2013 Oct 54(5): 423-31.

Fitzsimons, Grainne, Chartrand, Tanya, Fitzsimons, Gavan. Automatic effects of brand motivated behavior: How Apple makes you "Think Different." *Journal of Consumer Research.* 2018, March 4.

Fox, Glenn; Kaplan, Jonas; Damasio, Hanna; Damasio, Antonio. Neural correlates of gratitude. *Frontiers in Psychology.* 2015; 6: 1491.

Fox GR, Sobhani M, Aziz-Zadeh L. Witnessing hateful people in pain modulates brain activity in regions associated with physical pain and reward. *Frontiers in Psychology.* 2013 Oct 23;4:772.

Fulghum, Robert. *All I Really Need to Know I Learned in Kindergarten, 2004.*

Gino, Francesca and Grant, Adam. The big benefit of a little thanks. *Harvard Business Review.* November, 2013.

Grant AM, Gino F. A little thanks goes a long way: Explaining why gratitude expressions motivate prosocial behavior. *Journal of Personality and Social Psychology.* 2010 Jun;98(6):946-55.

Greenberg, David. *Presidential Doodles: Two Centuries of Scribbles, Squiggles, Scratches & Scrawls from the Oval Office,* 2007.

Gottman, John. https://www.gottman.com/

Haidt, Jonathan. *The Happiness Hypothesis: Finding Modern Truth in Ancient Wisdom.* Basic Books. 2006.

Haselhuhn, Michael P.; Schweitzer, Maurice E. and Kray, Laura, Beyond Belief: How Implicit Beliefs Influence Trust (April 15, 2008). Available at https://ssrn.com/abstract=1124591

Hershfield, Hal. You make better decisions if you see your senior self. *Harvard Business Review.* June, 2013.

Hsu, D.T., Sanford, B.J., Meyers, K.K. et al., Response of the u-opioid system to social rejection and acceptance. *Molecular Psychiatry* 18. August, 2013.

Isaacson, Walter. *Einstein,* 2011.

Jacob, Bert and Jacobs, John. *Life is Good, 2015.*

Johnstone, Brick; Holliday, Greyson; Cohen, Daniel. Heightened religiosity and epilepsy: evidence for religious-specific neuropsychological processes. *Mental Health, Religion & Culture.* 2016; 19 (7): 704

Kahneman, Daniel. *Experienced Utility and Objective Happiness: A Moment-Based Approach* in Choices, Values and Frames. (2000).

Kahneman, Daniel. *Thinking Fast and Slow.* Farrar, Straus and Giroux. 2013.

Kirby, Elizabeth, Daniela ,Kaufer, et. al., Acute stress enhances adult rat hippocampal neurogenesis and activation of newborn neurons via secreted astrocytic FGF2. Published online; eLife 2013;2:e00362 DOI: 10.7554/eLife.00362

Klein, Gary. *Seeing What Others Don't.* Public Affairs, 2013.

Laham, Simon; Koval, Peter; Alter, Adam. The name-pronounciation effect: Why people like Mr. Smith more than Mr. Colquhoun. *Journal of Experimental Social Psychology.* 2011, June 11.

Lally, Phillipa; Gardner, Benjamin; Wardle, Jane. Making health habitual: the psychology of 'habit-formation' and general practice. *British Journal of General Practice.* 2012 Dec; 62(605): 664-666.

Leary, Mark; Diebels, Kate; Davisson, Erin; Jongman-Sereno, Katrina; Isherwood, Jennifer; Raimi, Kaitlin; Deffler, Samantha; and Hoyle, Rick. "Cognitive and Interpersonal Features of Intellectual Humility," *Personality and Social Psychology Bulletin,* March 17, 2017. DOI: 10.1177/0146167217697695.

Loewenstein, George. Out of control: Visceral influences on behavior. *Organizational Behavior and Human Decision Processes.* 1996, March. Vol. 65. No. 3.

Losada, Marcial and Heaphy, Emily. The role of positivity and connectivity in the form of business teams. Published online February 1, 2004: doi.org/10.1177/0002764203260208

Luna, Tania and Renninger, Tania. *Surprise: Embrace the Unpredictbale and Engineer the Unexpected,* 2015.

Lyubomirsky, Sonja. The Greater Good Science Center, http://greatergood.berkeley.edu/author/sonja_lyubomirsky

Maguire, EA; Woollett K, and Spiers, HJ. London taxi drivers and bus drivers: a structural MRI and neuropsychological analysis. *Hippocampus.* 2006;16(12):1091-101.

McCullough, Michael; Orsulak, Paul; Brandon, Anna; Akers, Linda. Rumination, fear, and cortisol: An in vivo study of interpersonal transgressions. *Health Psychology,* Vol 26(1), Jan 2007, 126-132

Moscovici, S., & Zavalloni, M. (1969). The group as a polarizer of attitudes. *Journal of Personality and Social Psychology, 12*(2), 125-135.

Over, Harriet; Carpenter, Malinda. Evidence that priming affiliation increases helping behavior in infants as young as 18 months. *Association for Psychological Science.* 2009, September 9.

Packard, Vance. *Hidden Persuaders.* Ig Publishing, 1959

Paterniti, Michael. *Driving Mr. Albert: A Trip Across America.* Dial Press, 2001.

Polage, Danielle. Making up History: False memories of fake news stories. *Europe's Journal of Psychology.* 2012, Vol. 8(2), 245-250.

Roberts, Siobhan "A Hands-On Approach to Studying the Brain, Even Einstein's". *The New York Times*, 14 November, 2006.

Rohde, Mike. *The Sketchnotes Handbook: The Illustrated Guide to Visual Notetaking*, 2012.

Schkade, David; Sunstein, Cass; and Reid Hastie. What Happened on Deliberation Day, 95 Cal. L. Rev. 915 (2007).

Seligman, Martin. *Learned Optimism: How to Change Your Mind and Your Life,* Vintage Publications, 2006.

Senn Delaney. Why fostering a growth mindset in organizations matters. available online: http://knowledge.senndelaney.com/docs/thought_papers/pdf/stanford_agilitystudy_hart.pdf

Shenhav, Amitai; Rand, David; and Greene, Joshua. Divine intuition: Cognitive style influences belief in God. *Journal of Experimental Psychology.* 2011, August 8. DOI: 10.1037/a0025391

University of Utah Health Sciences. "This is your brain on God: Spiritual experiences activate brain reward circuits." *ScienceDaily.* 2016, November.

Weiwei Men, et al., "The corpus callosum of Albert Einstein's brain: another clue to his high intelligence?" *Brain,* 2014, April 137(4).

Weir, Kirsten. The pain of social rejection. *American Psychological Association, Science Watch.* 2012, Vol. 43. No. 4.

Winkielman, Piotr and Cacioppo, John. Mind at ease puts a smile on the face: Psychophysiological evidence that processing facilitation elicits positive affect. *Journal of Personality and Social Psychology.* 2001, Vol. 81, No. 6.

Witelson, Sandra. "The exceptional brain of Albert Einstein". *Lancet.* Volume 353 (9170): 2149–53.

Zolli, Andrew and Healy, Ann Marie. *Resilience: Why Things Bounce Back.* Simon & Schuster, 2013.